TOWNS AND BUILDINGS

Steen Eiler Rasmussen

TOWNS AND BUILDINGS

DESCRIBED IN DRAWINGS AND WORDS

THE MIT PRESS
Cambridge, Massachusetts

First Danish edition 1949
First English edition 1951
First MIT Press paperback edition, March 1969
Second printing, September 1973
Third printing, April 1979

Illustrations and typography by the author.
Photographed from the English edition and
printed and bound in the United States of America
by Halliday Lithograph Corp.

ISBN 0 262 68011 4 (paperback)
Library of Congress catalog card number: 69-13127

PREFACE

An unusual house in a street attracts attention but no impression remains of the street in its entirety. For though it is easy to discover a particular detail, it is very difficult to grasp the whole, no matter how simple it is. This interest in isolated details, which is natural to most people, is further stimulated by their reading. Innumerable books are written on historical styles, books purporting to show how the creations of various periods can be distinguished from one another by small, seemingly insignificant traits. And as a matter of fact it can be quite exciting to be able to decide, like an antiquarian, to which epoch of cultural history some lovely thing belongs. It can become a veritable mania just as the study of perforations and misprints can be for the stamp collector.

The ability to identify and classify architecture is often useful when travelling and there are travel guides to point out the museums one should visit and every item in them considered worth seeing. These guides also enumerate all the buildings the tourist is supposed to admire. Such books are compiled for the type of traveller who, one imagines, goes through strange cities as though they, too, were museums, taking note of the three-starred numbers. But the cities, themselves, they do not see any more than they see the museum rooms in which the works of art are found.

There are excellent German and Japanese guide books giving detailed information about every single palace and temple in Peking. But they do not contain a single mention of the fact that the entire city is one of the wonders of the world, in its symmetry and clarity a unique monument, the culmination of a great civilization. T h a t we must discover for ourselves. And the nine-sided town of Palma Nuova, which, in its geometrical form, is as fine as an ice crystal, is noted in the Italian Baedeker simply as a fortified town.

In the present book an effort has been made to bring the reader to look on the city as an entity which expresses certain ideals. The individual monuments, the buildings, thus become part of a whole. The cities are not all treated in the same fashion or according to a particular method. The chapters are as varied as the subjects, for there are no two cities in the world that are identical. In some instances it has seemed natural to begin by drawing up the main lines, which have determined the arrangement of all else, and then to go on to the details; the monumental buildings, the ordinary houses and the streets. In other cases it seemed more fitting to begin with a particular monument which had been a determining factor in the formation of its surroundings, the nucleus from which all the rest evolved. In some cases much can be learned by observing common traits in cities which came into existence under the same conditions and for the same reasons; in others it is necessary to seek the clue to a unique development.

To make similarities or contrasts easier to comprehend, most of the town plans are reproduced to the same scale, 1:20.000. It is interesting to compare the size of ancient Greek and Roman cities with medieval towns and with familiar elements, such as the street net of a modern city. Unfortunately it has not been possible to carry out this principle in all cases as the great cities of today are so unreasonably vast that no book, whatever its format, would be able to contain comparisons of them with towns of earlier days. But by employing simple scale measurements and then, as for example in the case of Paris, reducing the scale to half size and again to a fifth, it should be possible to maintain a basis of comparison.

A number of famous places are drawn to a scale of 1:2000 so that direct comparison can be made between an ancient Greek market-place and Rome's Capitol or Copenhagen's Amalienborg Place.

The buildings described in this book are not treated as monuments to be seen from the outside, only. Architecture creates rooms for people to live and move about in. Though the façade is, of course, an important part of the building, it is nevertheless only the outward expression of something very complicated which cannot be understood before we have perceived the relation between the interior and the exterior, between the human existence around which the house is built and the technical resources available at the time of its construction. It is difficult to give an impression of these things by means of illustrations. Technically we say that a building is determined by drawings of plan, section and façades and that these must harmonize well if it is to be good architecture. But such descriptions, which are quite clear to architects, make no appeal to the imagination. On the other hand, no photographs or other pictorial presentation of the interior and exterior of a building, regardless of the wealth of the material, can give any impression of the relation of the rooms to each other and of all of them to the massive block of the building. Therefore a new method of illustration has been attempted in this book. In several instances the building is shown at the top of the page, e n f a c e, in perspective, as it would appear to an observer standing before it; beneath this and corresponding to it we see the building as it would present itself if, like a doll's house, the front wall could be removed to reveal the rooms behind the façade. In this way we discover what is hidden behind the windows and doors of the exterior. Beneath this section, which gives a better idea of the interior than an ordinary scaled drawing of a section, we see how the house would look if the upper storeys could be lifted off so that we could peer down to the ground-floor and study the disposition of the principle rooms.

This mathematically clear presentation in all its factual sobriety is in keeping with an aspect of architecture which other kinds of illustrations could hardly demonstrate. It also has the advantage of being easy to grasp. Even children like it. They love to see "what is inside" and can imagine themselves walking about the rooms of the building. It has the further advantage of compressing into one page information which otherwise would fill many more and it has been the particular aim of the author, ever since the planning of the book, to put a great deal of material into a modest amount of space. However, as illustrations of this kind demand much expensive drawing work, it would have been impossible to carry out the book with its many original drawings if the N e w C a r l s b e r g F o u n d a t i o n of Copenhagen had not so generously defrayed the expenses of both art work and plates for the original Danish edition.

Accurately scaled drawings, however, cannot give a complete picture of architecture. When the Danish edition of the book was planned in 1945 the possibilities of procuring good paper for difficult reproductions were few; therefore it was decided to illustrate the work solely with line drawings which make small demands on the paper's quality. To these scaled drawings it was possible to add reproductions of engravings and woodcuts as well as unpretentious sketches and outline drawings. The result is a rather heterogeneous collection of illustrations and some of the sketches may seem rather unessential and vague compared to the very exact architectural drawings and plans. It is, however, the author's hope that the reader will accept them as enlivening titbits — a marginal note here, a hasty travel reminiscence there and, again, a small vignette which the author has been tempted to place in the margin when he felt that words, alone, could not express the feelings and impressions he wished to share with the reader.

Good reproductions of photographs would, in many cases, be better but they would also require much more space if they were to reveal as much. But, as already mentioned, the aim has been not to expand the book but to pack it tightly with matter pertaining to cities and buildings — not in a systematic presentation of the history of town planning and architecture but in an informal series of chapters on subjects which, the author feels, it was fun to work with. And it is his hope that the book will give the interested reader some fresh impressions just as on a journey during which we now discover entirely new things, now find new meaning in old, familiar things.

This English edition is different from the Danish original. The author has attempted to bring more harmony to the length and contents of the chapters without changing the general character of the book. Some chapters have been shortened, others have been given a fuller form. The one on the Dutch contribution is new. The author has worked in close co-operation with Mrs. Eve Wendt who made the translation and took great pains in transferring into English the very style and spirit of the book. He is also most grateful to Flora and Gordon Stephenson for valuable advice and for their careful reading of manuscript and proofs. The interest and skill which the blockmaker and the printer have shown in the rather exacting task has been a special pleasure to

Steen Eiler Rasmussen.

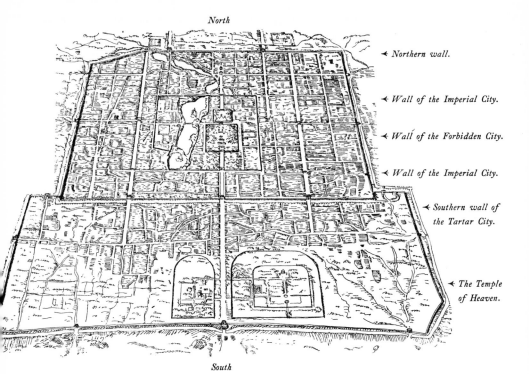

◄ *Northern wall.*

◄ *Wall of the Imperial City.*

◄ *Wall of the Forbidden City.*

◄ *Wall of the Imperial City.*

◄ *Southern wall of*
the Tartar City.

◄ *The Temple*
of Heaven.

South

THE CITY A TEMPLE

Peking, the capital of old China! Has there ever been a more majestic and illuminative example of sustained town-planning?

It was a city of a million inhabitants but quite different from our idea of a metropolis. For miles on end the living-quarters consisted of grey, one-storeyed houses lying along narrow, dusty-grey roads behind walls over which rose the tops of green trees. It was like a village, but a village out of all proportion — three miles in one direction and five miles in the other. Yet co-existent with the village-like aspect of the residential sections there was a grandeur in the lay-out of the entire city not to be found in any European capital. Following a clear principle, straight highways, broader than the Paris boulevards, run through the whole town.

Peking is built up according to a system of rules which, to a European, seems half mysticism, half common-sense. But neither of these terms is really adequate; the ideas and convictions of a culture like the Chinese can never be completely explained by words derived from a culture like ours.

I

In many parts of Denmark a fixed tradition has been handed down from one generation to another as to the orientation of houses in the landscape. There is nothing strange in this. On the west coast of Jutland, for example, and indeed all the way down along the coast of the North Sea right into the north of France, all houses are built in long, parallel wings, squatting down behind the dune rows to avoid as much as possible the clutches of the fierce west wind. It is just as sensible that the Chinese, in so far as they are able, place their buildings so that they open toward the south; for in a climate where the sun is very potent and stands high in the heavens a southern exposure with large, projecting roofs over the buildings is the best. But just as old home remedies — which on closer examination prove to be sensible enough — are often hedged in with a lot of abracadabra, Chinese building principles, sensible in themselves, are often based on ideas concerning the influence of heaven and earth, evil spirits, etc.. Thus, imperceptibly, they pass over to other principles completely outside the control of reason — the sort of principles which we have in Europe particularly in connection with temples and churches. Since early times, for instance, it has been imperative that our churches be built with the chancel at the east end. This is not founded on common-sense. It is ritual. For the Chinese all building practice was, really, ritual, and if there were no established rules for a given case the priests, who were deemed to be in intimate contact with the powers that govern nature, would have to be consulted. And when every house and every temple had to be built according to ritual, how much more important this must have been for the laying out of the main city of the entire empire! For Peking was much more than a capital. It was the residence of the emperor and the emperor was more than a regent or a sovereign; he was a demigod. "The Son of Heaven" he was called and had the functions of supreme pontiff. Every year at midwinter it was his prerogative to make the great sacrifices to heaven which re-established the pact between man and the Omnipotent and insured a good year. He succeeded in making himself the spiritual head of his people. His throne was a sanctuary, the throne hall a temple facing due south, the entire city a temple ground.

The Imperial Palaces are admirably illustrated by drawings and photographs in Oswald Sirén: Imperial Palaces of Peking I-III, 1926.

City wall and canal surrounding Peking.

Peking's most important feature was the great Processional Road, a Via Sacra paved with broad, hewn flags, which led from the throne hall directly south to that part of the city where the Temples of Heaven and Agriculture lay. *See drawing, p. 4.*

In its plan Peking is very reminiscent of Babylon as described by Herodotus (about 450 B.C.), another city which had been equally important as capital, trade centre and temple. According to Herodotus it was a large, regular, walled town built round a Processional Road leading from the palace to the main temple. Recent excavations, however, have proved that his description was somewhat idealized. But in Peking the ideal city became reality. Coming with the camel caravans out of the plains and approaching its great old walls, *R. Koldewey: Das wieder erstehende Babylon. 1913.* you see before you a veritable scene from the Old Testament. Flocks of sheep graze peacefully along the canals which, moat-like, surround the city. Within, Peking appears as one square town placed inside another until the holy of holies is reached — "the Forbidden City" where the emperor resided and where no intruder could force his way. In contrast to the colourless residential sections with their grey walls and grey roofs, "the Forbidden City" glitters with red plastered walls, many-coloured woodwork and roofs of glazed ochre tiles — ritual again: only the emperor's buildings could have yellow roofs. While it was called by Europeans the Forbidden City, its Chinese name was the Purple City. This name, *Tzu Chin Ch'eng,* has nothing to do with the colour of its crenellated walls but is purely symbolical. It is an allusion to the "purple

For Peking walls see: The Walls and Gates of Peking by Oswald Sirén, London, 1924, with excellent illustrations.

3

The great Processional Road looking toward the entrance to the Forbidden City.

polar star", centre of the celestial world, as the Imperial Palace was the centre round which the terrestrial world gravitated. Thus both Confucius and Laotse speak of the emperor's position. The Purple City is built symmetrically about the great north-south axis with large reception halls and courts containing apartments for the emperor's concubines and eunuchs and an enormous court staff. Outside its walls lies the "Imperial City", also surrounded by walls and also a court city. But within its domain is a special precinct — surrounded by walls of its own — called the Sea Palaces, a fantastic park containing three artifical lakes, with artifical mountains and grottoes, temples and pavilions and houses, where the emperor could live like a philosopher amid natural surroundings — natural surroundings designed and made by man!

Compare with plan, p. 29.

The White Dagoba crowning a little artificial mountain at the northernmost end of the Sea Palaces.

The whole of Peking has been fitted into nature by being given great symmetry. The city itself is an image of nature's undeviating regularity as the astronomer knows it. But the Sea Palaces also represent a special interpretation of nature, the interpretation of the painter and poet which is not dependent on anything so simple as rules. The moment you set foot inside the walls of the Sea Palaces you feel as though you have been transported to a fabulous place far out in the country. From the West Mountains, which from Peking are seen as a blue silhouette, water has been brought through canals to the city for the moats and the large artificial lakes. The soil which was removed to make the northernmost lake has been formed into a pleasant little mountain which is crowned by a bottle-

*The northernmost of the lakes
in the gardens of the Sea
Palaces, "Pei Hai", seen
from an artificial mountain
north of the Forbidden City.
At left, the little mountain
with the White Dagoba.*

shaped pagoda, the White Dagoba as Europeans call it, a
monument for a Buddhistic relic. A bridge leads to it. From
the pagoda there is an excellent view over the city, and up
here even the symmetrical Purple City appears irregular because it is seen from a corner. The great city of a million
souls seems to be one huge park for in the glimmer of the
sun's rays the view is dominated by the many green trees
which overshadow the small, grey houses. Only the gateway
towers and the high roofs of the Forbidden City stand out
clearly. Up here on the mountain the sun is baking and
throws back glaring reflections from the mirror of the
lakes. Under leafy trees winding paths lead down its slope.
At one spot you find an open wooden gallery through which
winged insects fly. It has a tiled floor and in one corner
there is an opening with a stairway that seems to descend
right into the heart of the mountain. But after a turn the
dark, cool grotto ends in a circular wooden pavilion resting
on the side of the mountain with a broad view over the lake
to the far distant shore. Groping your way further down the
slope you reach a little flagged terrace where you discover a
stone turtle with a tall stone tablet standing on its back and,
further still, you come to a long, curved wooden gallery edging
the lake. Low skiffs sail among the lotus over to the other
shore which is a legendary world of tea pavilions, strange
temples, bridges and galleries, weird rock gardens, and all the
rest that a Chinese imagination can invent, executed with
great elaborateness. It is that Chinese culture we know so well

5

One of the larger dwellings of Peking, consisting of a number of houses and court-yards. It is exactly orientated in relation to a north-south axis. But the entrance (at bottom of drawing) is placed to one side of the axis. This is a fixed principle: evil spirits must not be able to rush straight into the house. Note that the northern gates of Peking are not placed opposite the southern gates.

from oriental porcelain, embroideries and painting, and which has inspired Europeans to bring forth a thousand chinoiseries until at last it has come to represent to us the very quintessence of Chinese being. How doubly surprising it is, then, when we come out of the enchanted world of the Sea Palaces into the everyday greyness of Peking to discover that it is classical and regular, so completely lacking in all that which we mean by chinoiserie!

The great main highways are very broad avenues with a roadway in the middle for all through traffic. On each side of it there is an equally broad thoroughfare which partly serves as what we call the sidewalk, partly is used for more local traffic, partly is an area for all sorts of outdoor work. It is an excellent arrangement. Shops and work-rooms are open booths which almost merge into the street where the Chinese display their wares, shoe horses, hold their pig market, let their tired camels sink heavily down to rest, fetch up the water from the public wells, are shaved and trimmed by the street barber, and carry on a hundred and one other things. Originally the middle roadway was reserved for the emperor's officials, the mandarins. Everything, indeed, had its purpose in relation to the imperial residence. For instance, the reason why houses could be only one storey high was so that no one could see over the walls of the Forbidden City.

From the broad highways run the narrow residential streets where there are no shops. There may be houses which reflect the whole plan of Peking with everything carefully orientated in relation to a north-south axis and with several courtyards, one behind the other. There may also be unsymmetrical Chinese gardens behind symmetrical groups of buildings. But seen from the street there is hardly any difference to be noted between a large, costly mansion or a cluster of coolie hovels. One sees only grey walls without windows, with here and there an entrance. Just as no one may look over the walls of the Imperial City, no one may compete with the magnificence of the imperial palace. In the small, narrow streets there are no shops. But they are visited by many dealers carrying their wares. Each one calls attention to himself by means of some small instrument, a long tuning-fork, small brass bowls which are sounded against each other something like castanets, small flutes; all make delicate sounds that are heard behind the walls in faint tones which announce to the listener who it is that is passing.

It is an existence and a world very different from ours. And yet it is of great interest to us, not as a curiosity but as the most fully developed example of a special city type which arises when a ruler makes himself a high-priest or a deity for his people. Of itself a ritual develops which forms the city. When the French monarch became absolute a system of rules and regulations evolved governing his conduct and the conduct of those surrounding him, and it was logical that he should live in a city which was just as systematically built up around the king. And when the Third Reich was created with Hitler as a leader who was a godhead for his people, it was necessary to form German city-planning according to special rites, with axes and halls and processional roads.

Residential streets "Hutungs" in Peking. The street is not paved, only a dusty grey road between grey houses with here and there a large green tree seen above the walls. Lean black pigs gallop through the streets and in the summer well-built, stark-naked children play in them with no unnecessary noise while the tradesmen pass through the streets producing their delicate, elfin-like music.

7

COLONIAL CITIES

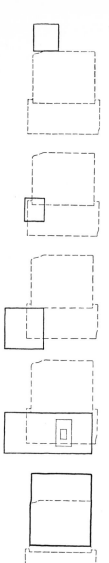

The cities on the site of Peking:

1) Chi, destroyed 221 B. C.
2) Yen, 70—936. 3) Yen-Ching, 936—1125. 4) Chung Tu, 1125—1268. 5) Kublai Khan's city, T'aitu, founded 1268.

It is not only when a city is made into a temple that it becomes regular. If a group of people leave their native soil and find themselves suddenly faced with the necessity of creating a new town in a strange place they must build it according to a preconceived plan or it will end in chaos. And that plan must, of necessity, be a very simple one, easily laid out, so that everyone with the least possible trouble can quickly discover what he has to do. Soldiers pitch camp by raising their tents in long, straight rows within a regular area so that sentry duty and defence are the easiest possible. Even nomadic tribes arrange their tents in accordance with simple camp plans.

When you gaze across the Forbidden City from one of the artificial mountains in Peking, its curved Chinese roofs seem to resemble a petrified tent city. The layout of modern Peking is based on a plan of 1268 when Kublai Khan, the great Mongolian emperor, founded his symmetrical capital. As the Mongols are still a warrior and nomadic people it is not difficult to understand why Europeans believe they can see in Peking's plan an outgrowth of the military encampment, the garrison town. But it is doubtful whether this is correct. Almost nothing can be concluded from the fact that the buildings resemble tents. At any rate, they are not in the least like *Mongolian* tents, which are stretched over a framework so that they appear convex, not concave. When he became emperor, Kublai Khan took over much of the *Chinese* culture and the Chinese have been settled farmers as far back as their history can be traced. There where he built his residential city five different towns had existed, one after the other, over a period of thousands of years; each one perfectly rectangular and each one orientated exactly north-south and east-west. When you know how difficult it is to lay out a city accurately orientated you are aware that it is never done for *practical* reasons. And when you hear why the cities were moved from one place to another right beside it, it will be quite clear that it had no practical purpose in any sober sense of the term. The Venetian merchant, Marco Polo, who visited China from 1275 to 1292, at the time of Kublai Khan, wrote on returning home: "Now there was on that spot in old times a great and noble city, called Cambaluc, which is as much as to say in our tongue 'The City of the Emperor'. But the great Kaan was informed by his Astrologers that this city would prove rebellious and raise great disorders against his imperial authority. So he caused the present city to be built close beside the old one with only a river between them. And caused the people of the old city to be removed to the new town that he had founded."

In ancient times there were undoubtedly certain rites in connection with every large undertaking; it has not been possible to discriminate clearly between ritual forms and purely practical ones. Nevertheless, it is probably justifiable to distinguish between towns which, like Peking, became out-and-out temple cities, their layout determined by priests and astrologers; and, on the other hand, more practical settlements such as colonial cities or garrison towns.

Modern technique, which has facilitated the rapid transport of goods over great distances, has made it possible for cities to continue expanding without form or bounds. But in ancient times a city could only grow to a certain size dependent on the ability of a rather limited agricultural district to furnish food for it. If the population became too large the choice for the surplus was either starvation or emigration — and naturally they chose the latter. The world was wide then and there was much virgin soil where people could settle and form new towns. Almost the same story can be told to describe the expansion of the Greeks from their barren native shores over the islands and coasts of the Mediterranean or, much later, the eastward migration of the Germans of the Middle Ages or, later still, the emigration of Europeans to America.

At first the Greeks were (like the Norsemen before the Viking Age) dependent on the trading genius of another people, the Phoenicians, who brought their wares to Greece. But as time went by the Greeks, themselves, developed into a sea-faring nation and they were not content with visiting the ports of others. The two hundred years from the middle of the 8th century to the middle of the 6th century B. C. formed an uninterrupted period of Greek expansion. This mighty colonization was by no means the result of a premeditated trade policy. It was just as much a natural phenomenon as it is when a tree scatters its seed and a copse grows up.

The present Peking in outline (drawn to the same scale as the old cities, p. 8, where it is sketched in with a dotted line). At top, the Tartar city, surrounding the Imperial City which likewise surrounds the Forbidden City. Below, the Chinese city with the two large enclosures, the Temples of Agriculture and Heaven; the two cities connected by the north-south axis.

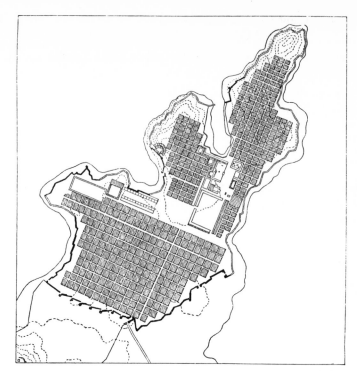

Plan of Miletus.
Scale 1 : 20.000.
North upward.

See: How the Greeks built
Cities, by R. E. Wycherly.
London. 1949.

See Armin von Gerkan:
Griechische Städteanlagen,
p. 42 et. seq.

The southernmost part of the
plan is Roman and has, as
can be seen, larger squares
than the Greek part.

The colonies were all city-states like the mother community. All Greek states were, according to our idea, small. Ten to twenty thousand inhabitants was probably the maximum.

The plans of the older Greek towns were irregular. But later they began laying out their cities in squares. On the basis of a statement by Aristotle it was formerly thought that the gridiron plan was invented, so to speak, by one man. His name is *Hippodamos of Miletus* and he lived in the 5th century B. C. Now it is believed, however, that the regular city plan was a practical measure which developed of itself, as is always apparent in colonial cities, and that Hippodamos' contribution was, rather, to form a theory from it and put it into practice.

Miletus, itself, — the town that fostered Hippodamos — was an Ionian city on the west coast of Asia Minor and it was the starting point of a gigantic colonization. At least sixty colonies originated from there. Compared to its colonies the city was old-fashioned. But when it was rebuilt after being razed by the Persians in the 5th century, it was made completely regular. Miletus prospered even more under the Romans. It grew to be a city of 80-100,000 inhabitants.

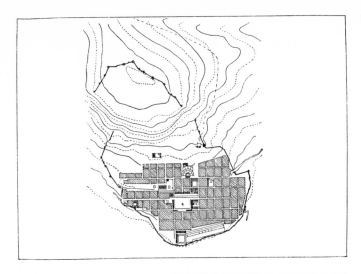

Plan of Priene.
Scale 1 : 20.000.
North upward.

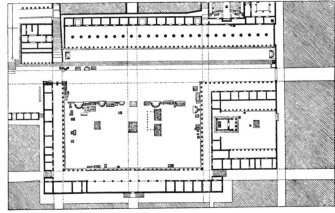

Priene's Agora.
Scale 1 : 2.000.

North of Miletus high above the Maeander Plain, lay
Priene, also regularly laid out and with its rocky soil formed in
terraces. The streets were laid from east to west to assure the
minimum of gradient. They were about 20-foot broad, paved
with light-coloured stone. At right angles to them ran the
10-foot cross streets, with steps. The housing blocks were rectangular, normally with four building sites to each. In such
a city not only were building plots of equal size provided for
each family but there were also various large establishments
for the use of the entire community. In the centre of the plan,
adjoining the main street, lies the market place, the town's
Agora. The city also had its temples and, at the foot of the
mountain its *stadion* and *gymnasion,* where fresh mountain
water spouted out of the lion heads in the marble walls.

11

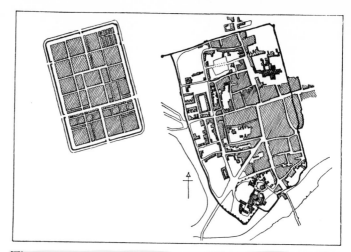

The English city of Chester.
Scale 1 : 20.000.
North upward.
At left, the rectangular Ro-
man city, to the right, the
city as it is today with a me-
dieval wall which, to the
north and east, almost fol-
lows the Roman.

The market place is like a beautiful pillared assembly hall open to the heavens. Originally there were colonnades on all four sides for booths but later a Maecenas broke up the symmetry of the square by adding the large, two-naved hall of columns north of the market place; a sacred hall, broader than the square, a gathering place where the citizens could gossip with friends while strolling in the shade. It was a community centre, a sort of town hall. The small cells in the rear were offices for the city administration.

The Mediterranean coast was the colonizing area of the Greeks. When their time came the Romans were to dominate large parts of Europe. Their colonial towns were not, like the Greek, the result of the emigration of people for whom there was not enough room at home. They were, above all, garrison towns to guard strategically important crossings in conquered territory. (The Romans had just reached the point in technique and administration where they could permit a few towns to expand to what we would consider large cities — with all the evils that follow in their train. Rome knew — as well as we do today — slum districts with wretched tenement houses and a dangerous proletariat.) From as far away as England all roads led to Rome and it was vital that they

English towns with names
ending in -chester were ori-
ginally a Roman camp: Ca-
strum.

be nowhere cut off by the oppressed peoples. Therefore it was necessary to have garrison towns to protect every vulnerable point. A free passage for the legions to all parts of the empire was always necessary. Every city was a military encampment, a *castrum*. All English towns ending in -chester originate from

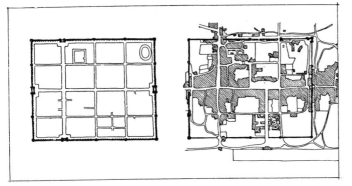

Aosta.
Scale 1 : 20.000.

The drawing at the left shows the Roman city, to the right is the plan of the city as it is today.

a Roman camp. In the plan of the city so laconically named Chester this can still be traced. Beyond the main street-crossings the towns might be variously laid out. These Roman garrison towns form the more or less clear nucleus of thousands of Europe's larger and smaller cities as we know them today. This is most clearly seen in cases where the towns have not expanded too greatly, such as Aosta.

Another city in Piedmont, Augusta Taurinorum, the present-day Turin, has greatly expanded since its Roman origin but has, like a crystal, steadily grown in accordance with the same geometric principle. The Renaissance added only its system of bastioned walls to the almost square Roman plan. Later, as a defensive measure, a strong citadel was built southwest of the city. Next followed, to the south, an irregular polygonal rampart but still with rectangular blocks within its walls. With the passing of time new additions in all directions stretched out the polygon more and more. The original eastern gateway lay finally almost in the middle of the city where a square was connected by a broad, arcaded street with the monumental Piazza S. Carlo to the south. The town continued to grow, adding one new rectangular block after the other until it became the great city which the 18th century Danish traveller and playwright, Ludvig Holberg, admired so greatly for its regularity.

Large, magnificent cities, like Timgad in Algiers, had entirely lost their importance and ceased to exist as cities by the early Middle Ages. Nevertheless, greater traces remain of them than of towns which continued to flourish because of the strategic and mercantile importance of their sites. They were continually rebuilt so that today nothing is left of the original

About Turino see : The Town Planning Review Vol. XII. 1927. p. 191 ff.

13

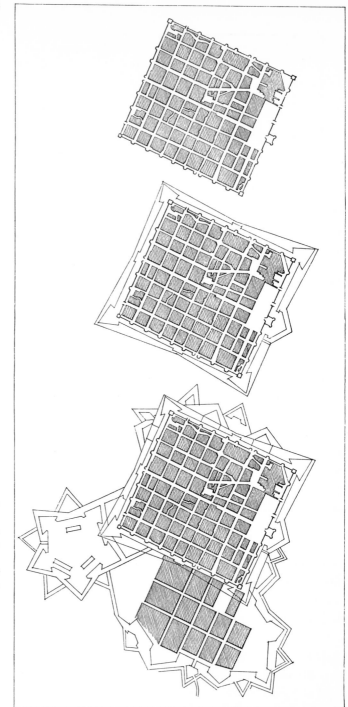

The city of Turin in five stages.
Scale 1 : 20.000.
North upward.
On this page from top to bottom:
1) The Roman city, Augusta Taurinorum. 2) Turin at the close of the 16th century. 3) Turin at the beginning of the 17th century with citadel and city extension.
On page 15:
4) Turin with a new extension from about 1670. 5) Turin at the end of the 17th century with still another extension, this time of the northwest.

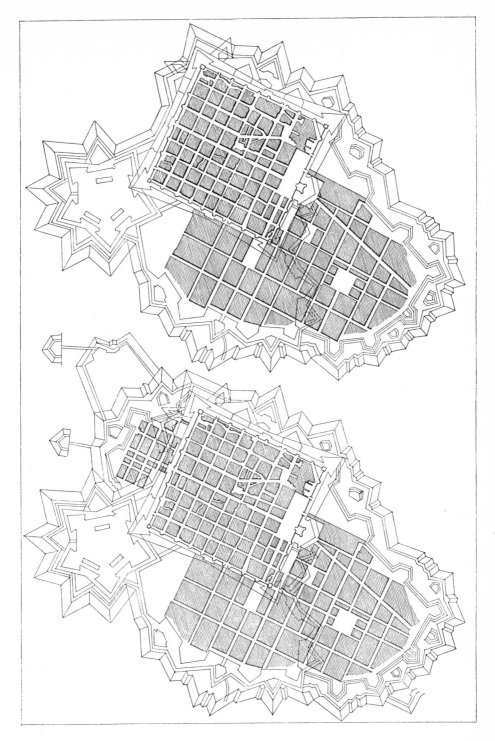

Cologne. A section of an engraving from the beginning of the 17th century. Below, on territory which in Roman times was under water, is seen around the Haymarket (B) Hanseatic district with gabled houses. Above (to the west) the medieval city which follows the lines of the old Roman town over which it is built.

towns. There was the important Rhine crossing where the Romans placed Colonia Agrippinensis on the western bank with a small fortification on the eastern shore. The city still bears in its name a reminiscence of the original Roman colony. The French and English call it Cologne, the Germans Köln and it has always been an important strategic centre. As early as the Middle Ages the Roman plan of Cologne was difficult to trace. In the same manner Roman towns lie hidden in Paris, London and Vienna.

It is usually believed that medieval cities developed very irregularly, without any plan. This is true of towns which grew slowly but it does not mean that irregularity was, somehow or other, an ideal of the time. When new towns were built rapidly the same method was employed as at all other times: they were laid out in rectangular blocks along straight streets. Here again it was the same story as in ancient Greece: when a city could no longer provide for more people some of the inhabitants left and founded new cities.

Between 1230 and 1300, for example, large colonies of Germans settled in Mecklenburg and Pomerania. A great number of quite regular towns were laid out, each one founded in a particular year. Excellent information is available as to where and how it happened. One of these German colonial towns is called New Brandenburg. We know that by letters patent, dated January 4, 1248, Markgraf Johann of Brandenburg authorized a certain knight, Sir Herbord, to build the town of New Brandenburg. Sir Herbord then induced a large number of people to settle there. This was not very difficult. At home in Brandenburg the younger sons of the peasantry had no prospects of ever getting their own farms. They would have to be farm hands all their lives. In the new town they would be given land, as such a colony was always started as a great agricultural undertaking. The new-comers settled in an untilled district thinly populated by a scarcely civilized people. The settlement was laid out as a market-town inside protective walls so that the intruders could live without fear of the natives. But the main occupation was agriculture. The inhabitants were given equally large pieces of ground to build on. This led to a square grid of rectangular blocks. There had to be a market-place. This was obtained by leaving one block unbuilt. There had also to be a church and churchyard. For these another block was taken. The city was not completely regular because the circular fortifications — probably constructed before anything else — cut off the blocks quite haphazardly. In this part of the country other cities from the same period are found within a few miles of each other, built in similar fashion. Few of them, however, are as regular as New Brandenburg. All of them vary more or less from the square grid, in each case due to geographical conditions.

Karl Wendt: Geschichte der Vorderstadt Neu Brandenburg. 1922. p. 4.

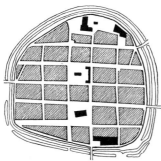

New Brandenburg.
Scale 1 : 20.000.
North upward.

17

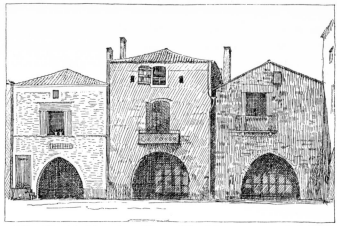

Houses on market-place in Monpazier.

The Danish town Køge in the 17th century. Scale 1 : 20.000. North upward.

Monpazier. Scale 1 : 20.000. North upward.

The Danish historian, Hugo Matthiessen, has pointed out that the town of *Køge,* on the island of Seeland in Denmark, which was established in the second half of the 13th century, is of the same type. And, indeed, the streets of New Brandenburg and Køge are very much alike. The building sites are quite large and the houses face the streets lengthwise while in many medieval commercial towns (e. g. the Hanseatic towns) the houses were built on narrow plots with high gables facing the streets. In the town of Køge, as in the German colonial towns, the market-place is separated from the church by a block but here it is safer from attack from outside than in New Brandenburg. Køge's market-place is just as well protected against enemy fire as the Chinese house against evil spirits.

One of the strangest examples of a very regular planned medieval town is Monpazier. It lies in the province of Guyenne in France, between the Dordogne and the Garonne. It was founded in 1284 by an *English* king who owned great stretches of present-day France. It is not only laid out in rectangular blocks and squares but its contours, too, — in contrast to the German colonial towns described above — are completely rectangular. The houses around the market-place are very narrow and all alike, and each one bestrides its street door in a broad, pointed arch so that together they form a delightful, shady arcade around the square.

When America was colonized the land there, too, was divided up in straight lines. The boundaries of the states are rectilineal and the networks of streets in the cities are just as regular as they were in the colonies of ancient Greece.

In town-planning the square grid, and in parcelling the rectangle, are still fundamental factors. The same general scheme has been followed even in cities founded in the 19th century. But it cannot be denied that it was best adapted to ancient and medieval towns which consisted entirely of homogeneous units. In our day there is decided differentiation. Some buildings are designed for dwelling purposes only, some for business and some for factories. Cities have no longer clear limits and, preferably, there should be recreation grounds in the city, itself, near the residential districts.

There is not very much information available about the greatest colonization project of the present day — the many new cities of the Soviet Union. But we do know that the Russians have been working with new principles. They have developed the theory of "the band city" in which the various elements are laid out in bands: the factories form one, park belts another, main traffic a third, the residential section a fourth. But just as the more or less square cities of the Middle Ages had to be altered to suit local conditions, the modern Russian band-city principle, too, must be adapted to the given circumstances.

THE IDEAL CITIES OF
THE RENAISSANCE

Centuries of great migrations and wars gave the feudal lord
in his castle a dominating position. To be able to lead a reason-
ably civilized life in the Middle Ages protection of one sort
or another was necessary. The master of the castle not only
protected the town from assault but also supplied it with its
means of existence.

It is easy to form an exaggerated idea of the amount of commerce carried on by the burgher towns and of the size of merchants' fortunes in those days. The towns engaged much more
in agriculture and handicrafts than in commerce as we know
it in modern cities. The men of property were the great lords
of the manors, temporal or spiritual, and they were, for the
most part, the ones who purchased the products of the towns.
It was the feudal lord who gave a town its fair and market
privileges. It was he who provided for the maintenance of
order on market days. He could muster the necessary man-
power to build castles and fortifications and to protect the
life of the town.

Through all this he had the power to determine the sites of
new cities. It might be a question of ordinary colonization, such
as at New Brandenburg (see page 17). Or military and political
motives might lie behind his decision. In the castles and towns
built by the Danish kings and their feudal lords about 1200,
a great national plan for the defence of the kingdom can be
seen. King Valdemar I (1157-1182), himself, fortified the
little island of *Sprogø,* strategically located in the middle of
the Great Belt between the islands of Seeland and Funen.

*Denmark with strongholds
of the Middle Ages. 1 Sprogø,
2 Havn now Copenhagen,
3 Århus, 4 Kalundborg.*

Bishop Absalon, his chancellor, built a citadel on an islet in the Sound just off the little trading and fishing village of *Havn* and fortified that small church town which later became the capital of the kingdom: Copenhagen. Traces of Absalon's stronghold are still found under Christiansborg Castle, the seat of government today. During the reign of King Valdemar's son, Canute VI, (1182-1202) another bishop, Peder Vagnssøn, founded the little town of St. Clemens, the heart of present-day Århus — Denmark's second-largest city — on the peninsula of Jutland, and probably laid the foundations for the still existent St. Clemens church, there. To protect the important Kattegat crossing to Jutland, Esbern Snare, like his brother Bishop Absalon the friend and foster-brother of King Valdemar I, built the town of Kalundborg with harbour and church on the northwestern coast of Seeland.

The upper town of Kalundborg to scale of 1 : 20.000, as it was in the Middle Ages. A hill town surrounded by walls, to the east protected by a large castle. The town itself is built around a square which, funnel-shaped, opens toward the 5-towered church.

Old Kalundborg was built on a hill, with a castle — no longer existent — at one end and a church at the other, a church which, with its five towers and loophole-like windows, was also a stronghold. It is quite evident that the town was planned, though it is not schematic, with its three-cornered square opening toward the church. The upper part is still one of the handsomest town units in Denmark.

In the medieval city the castle was one dominating factor and the church the other. The church was wealthy. The church was the important cultural link with the outside world, an international organism which has never been equalled since. And finally the church was the consolation and hope of the down-trodden masses who lived in the mean, small houses of the towns — the hope of a life hereafter better than the life of today.

Gradually, as payment-in-kind gave way to a money economy, the position of the towns changed. Commerce began to boom, the commoners became more and more conscious of their own strength and felt a growing independence of both temporal and spiritual powers. They were no longer willing to accept the hereafter as the essential meaning of life. People wanted to live here and now, they were more interested in their fellow-men than in angels. Natural sciences, based on mathematics, flourished. Society took over not only part of the power of the church but also some of its obligations.

21

See: Die Geschichte der Ideal-stadt by Georg Münter in the journal Städtebau 1929, page 249—56 and 317—340.

There arose the desire to create an ideal city, not as the background of a church or an adjunct to a castle, but as an independent and well-rounded whole for an ordinary civic community, well-protected against all aggressors, a classical Republic like the Greek city-states. The heathen philosophers of ancient Greece and Rome were studied for the knowledge and instruction that could not be found in the Bible.

The new weapons which followed on the invention of gunpowder created problems unknown to the colonial towns of the Middle Ages. Before the advent of gunpowder and cannonball, cities could be protected by palisades or walls. But now these were no longer enough. Earthworks were necessary. Attackers must be met with flanking fire. The castle acquired projecting towers and the ramparts were fitted with bastions.

The plans of Turin pp. 14 and 15 illustrate clearly how they developed from the Renaissance to the end of the 17th century. Pointed bastions have been added to the corners of the almost square Roman city. From these it was possible to send an enfilade along the sides of the ramparts. But the bastions, themselves, presented quite a large flank which also could be fired upon. Therefore they must be sharply pointed which technically is a poor form for earthern structures. It was quickly discovered that the rectangular contour was the least practical for a fortification of ramparts with bastions. A pentagon was better than a rectangle and a hexagon was still better. But best of all would be a town periphery in the form of a polygon.

A great amount of literature dealing with the new theory of fortifications appeared. Defences were a *sine qua non* for the existence of the city and if these were to form a polygonal rampart, cities, too, must be many-sided. Never before or since have so many projects for ideal cities been published.

The literature dealing with ideal cities first appeared in Italy. After 1600 it was Germany and France that took the lead. The great Italian artists of the Renaissance were, as is well-known, also superb technicians. Throughout the long period in which ideal projects were of such great interest there was no dividing line between art and technics. The artists loved applied mathematics and its beautifully exact results. Added to this came their knowledge of classical literature, the culture they wished to revive.

In a work on the theory of architecture from about 1500, by the Italian Francesco di Giorgio Martini, there are a number of ideal plans which seem to be children of the imagination of an extremely theoretical brain. Yet this same Francesco was actually a very practical man with wide experience both as architect and fortifications builder. And as a matter of fact his drawings were practical and real enough so that they might very well have served as models for many cities built according to similar schematic plans in the following centuries. As the drawings show, the determining factors in all of them were the fortification-polygon and the central square. The area between, Francesco sought to fill out in the best possible manner with a geometrical network of streets and squares. It is evident that he did not give much thought to the form of the houses or dwelling sites. Also in the medieval city a centrally located square had been a basic element, but nevertheless the forming of the house blocks was the primary interest while the squares and streets were simply spaces between them. In Francesco's plans the house blocks are the odds and ends remaining after the street network has been determined. This is clearly seen on the plan in which a thoroughfare is introduced as a spiral which crosses all the radial streets. Such a town plan has probably never been carried out but the two above it correspond to a number of actual cities of the 16th and 17th centuries.

Francesco also gives examples of plans for mountain towns. The mountain has been reduced to a skull-cap. Here, too, the streets are laid out in a very theoretical network which covers the spherical surface. These speculations, which undoubtedly were very natural for an Italian, probably never had any significance. Ideal cities were mostly carried out on level ground.

In *Braun und Hogenberg*'s Atlas, containing city plans from all over Europe, there is an engraving of an ideal city, Palma Nuova. This one was really built. Founded in 1593 in the state of Venice, it is one of the most intricate of all ideal cities. The polygonal rampart has nine sides and there are three gateways to the town. From them radial streets lead to the hexagonal square in the centre. The cross streets, lying in rings, correspond to the nine sides of the polygon and the

Plans for ideal cities by Francesco di Giorgio Martini, about 1500.

23

Plan for an ideal city — from Buonaiuto Lorini: "Delle fortificatione libri cinque". Venezia 1592.

Plan for an ideal city from Vincenzo Scamozzi: "Dell'idea dell' architettura universale". Venezia 1615.

Palma Nuova founded 1593, from an engraving by Braun & Hogenberg.

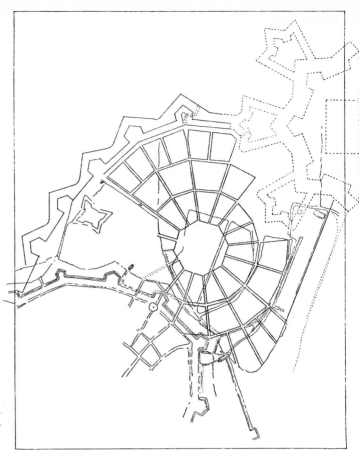

Proposal for a plan for the extension of Copenhagen, about 1629. Scale 1 : 20.000. North upward. Top, right: the Citadel, left: Rosenborg Castle. Below, left: The old City.

innermost ring of house blocks neutralizes the difference between the nine sides of the periphery and the six sides of the central *place*. The building in the centre, which resembles the castle in a game of chess, has never existed. As shown in the engraving there are also radial streets running from three of the bastions all the way to the centre. From the other six the streets extend only as far as the innermost ring street, ending in some sort of monumental gabled structure. The streets of Palma Nuova are actually laid out as shown in the engraving but their terminals are more casual. The rectangular spaces which are crossed by the middle ring street are also found in the town as small squares planted with trees. There is a book from about the same time as this city (1592) by an Italian, Buonaiuto Lorini, on fortification problems which also contains proposals for town plans. In it there is a drawing of a

See drawing page 24.

26

nine-sided city like Palma Nuova with radial streets and small
squares in a ring round a central *place*. But Palma Nuova's
plan with the three entrance highways leading to the heart of
the city is really handsomer.

A somewhat later ideal city plan (1615) which was never *See drawing page 24.*
carried out — drawn by Scamozzi — represents another prin-
ciple. All the blocks and squares are rectangular and all the
streets cross each other at right angles. Out toward the fortification-polygon the street blocks become irregular, arbitrarily
formed in triangles or other unsymmetrical shapes. In Lorini's
and Scamozzi's proposals we have the two basic types of ideal
plan. Either the polygonal rampart must determine the network of streets, which then will consist of ring streets parallel
with the line of fortifications and radial streets at right angles
to it, or one can work with a rectangular network haphazardly
cut off by the wall street.

King Christian IV of Denmark, who reigned from 1588 to
1648, founded a number of towns which were built in accordance with the ideals of the time. In a proposal for the expansion
of Copenhagen the polygonal town plan is found, featuring a
large octagonal place from which streets branch out to the
bastions of the fortifications. It could not be quite as regular
as ideal plans found in books for its form was dependent not
only on the existing city but on the coast line as well. However,
this proposal did not come into consideration in the final
disposition; a plan of the other type was chosen, with rectangular building sites between parallel streets. The same thing
happened when Christianshavn was built, a little town on the
island of Amager just opposite Copenhagen and now incorporated in the capital.

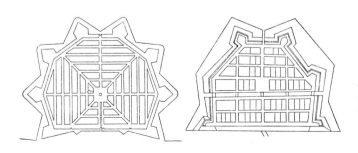

*At left: Johan Semp's pro-
posal for Christianshavn,
1617. Right: The plan used.
Scale for both about 1 : 20.000.*

27

THE GRAND PERSPECTIVE

Until quite recently history was regarded as the record of the lives of kings and great men transformed into popular drama with a small cast of outstanding figures, very much as in a play by Shakespeare. Today it is more usual to look on these individuals as tools of a development — generally an economic development — that is borne up by the nameless multitudes; and the course of this development is what we now mean by history. In other words, the conception of cause and effect has changed.

In the old days it would have been said that Sir Herbord founded New Brandenburg in 1248 (see p. 17) and, indeed, this was no myth as it could be documented; the letter existed which in one stroke brought the town of New Brandenburg into being. Today we would say that despite this fact the case is not so simple. The large population surplus in Brandenburg, itself, made emigration necessary. It was not by means of a letter, a sort of "open sesame", that the town was created by Sir Herbord. He was but the tool of forces stronger than any one man and the document was made effective by these forces. In much the same way it can be said of the ideal cities of the Renaissance that their outward form was logically determined by the laws of defence against the firearms of the day, so different from those that existed before the discovery of gunpowder. But there must have been someone who was the very first to make gunpowder and that inventor, that one person, was the one responsible for the revolutionary development. In the evolution of plants and animals there are mutations, sudden changes to new forms. In the same way there are mutations in human history. An idea of genius, the advancement of a thought never conceived before, inventions and discoveries — all these can lead economic development into new channels or quicken its course along the lines already laid out. The steam-engine did not *create* industrialism but it gave it immense impetus.

There are other inventions and discoveries which have not the slightest direct influence on economic development, on material history, but which can completely change the feeling for how things should be formed and in this way greatly influence cultural life, forms of expression. It is often the artist's achievement that he imagines and depicts that which becomes actual much later. Art can be like children's play: apparently without purpose or value and yet in the long run of greater importance than much so-called useful work.

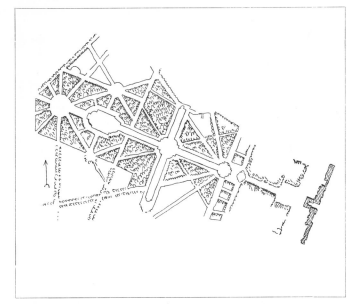

*Versailles Park.
Scale 1 : 40.000. North upward. At right, the palace, opposite it along the great axis of the park, the cross-shaped Grand Canal surrounded by pruned trees.*

Versailles is often pointed out as a logical manifestation of the absolute monarchy, a magnificent establishment which visibly demonstrates the central position of the ruler just as Peking did. But this does not explain the forms they have been given. These two particularly, Versailles and the Imperial Palaces of Peking, are worth comparing. At both places the huge grounds are laid out in artificial lakes, but how different they are! In Versailles the Grand Canal is an immense, symmetrically framed mirror of water which forms a splendid view from the centre of the palace and which continues along the symmetrical axis of the chateau almost to the horizon. In Peking the "Sea Palaces" are not smaller but they are formed in picturesque and capricious lakes which lay *beside* the axis of the symmetrical palace of the Forbidden City and quite independent of it. It is the private life of the emperor which here has found expression, literally speaking beside his official existence. Both parks are manifestations of artistic conceptions just as divergent as Chinese and French painting were around the year 1700.

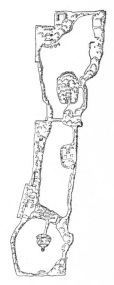

Peking, Sea Palace gardens. Scale 1 : 40.000. North upward. Compare p. 1.

29

*Landscape drawing by
Claude Lorrain.*

Chinese landscape drawing.

The Chinese paints almost as he writes. Just as he adds one character under another from top to bottom and lets each one mean a word or an idea, he paints one neat detail under the other and everyone understands that that which is painted at the top is that which is farthest away and that which is at the bottom is nearest to the observer. A French landscape drawing from the Versailles period, just like the Chinese, depicts lakes and mountains and human figures. But the landscape is seen stretching away *behind* the trees not, as in the Chinese picture, above them. A native of China would think it very wrong that the trees are shown becoming smaller and smaller the farther away they stand when everybody knows that they are more or less the same size. He would not understand this magical drawing in which everything not only loses in height in the background but also becomes lighter in colour until it almost vanishes in the airy silhouette of the farthest mountain. In the Chinese picture there are, quite logically, only two dimensions; paper is, after all, flat. The European picture gives the impression of a third dimension. The Chinese neither sees nor thinks in perspective.

No human being is born with the ability to experience the world around him in perspectives despite the fact that the picture which the retina of the eye receives *is* in perspective. If you stand in a street looking at a row of lamp-posts, the image on the retina will be in diminishing sizes, the nearest lamp-post largest, the most distant smallest. But you will not be fooled by this. You realize that they are all of the same size and that they stand behind each other. The discovery that an impression of perspective depth can be given by depicting things in gradually diminishing sizes revolutionized the art of reproducing that which is seen. This revolution in pictorial art occurred in Europe around 1400 but it never influenced China. European artists were so absorbed by it that they began to see the world around them in an entirely new light and it not only influenced their painting but also their idea of how buildings should be formed in relation to each other. The *vista* in town-planning came into existence.

In his theoretical work on "Geometry and Perspective" Albrecht Dürer has given a very clear description of the new theory. From various points on the mandolin to be sketched a string is drawn to a nail in the wall. From points at which the string intersects a plane determined by a frame, the distances to the edge of the frame are measured and marked off on a piece of paper, as shown in the illustration below. In this way a number of fixed points in the picture to be drawn are established. One can continue adding new points until an outline drawing in correct perspective is obtained.

This *was* a discovery! Now, 3-dimensional figures could be produced without having to model them, simply by drawing and painting them. It became a veritable sport to make them statuesque like real sculpture. It was not only possible to give the impression that they stood forth quite freely in space and

The theory of perspective illustrated in wood-cut by Albrecht Dürer.

31

Architectonic background from a mural painting by Pinturicchio in the library at Siena. Painted between 1502 and 1507.

The Tessin palace, Stockholm, 1694—97. Court looking toward pavilion at rear. The large colonnade seen at the top is only ostensibly very deep. Actually it is quite shallow but the columns in diminishing sizes give a splendid illusion of perspective depth.

formed on all sides, but it was even possible to compose architectural settings around them. Fantastical Renaissance buildings consisting only of colonnades and loggias and paved courts, which would be completely absurd as actual buildings, were given a sort of reality in the frescoes of the great painters. These decorations were employed to break through the walls of existing rooms, so to speak, so that they seemed to open on to the imaginary courts through whose arches and colonnades vistas of distant landscapes could be enjoyed. Ceilings were also painted with scenes which gave the illusion of openings to the skies, openings surrounded by balustrades over which happy mortals smiled down on the observer. In churches that could not afford real cupolas, paintings were carried out on the flat ceiling which, when seen from certain points on the floor, gave a perfect illusion of a domed roof. For great religious dramas scenery was painted in the form of grand architectural compositions in which the stories of the New Testament could be performed in appropriately magnificent settings.

In the courtyard of the Palazzo Spada in Rome an architectural jest is found in the form of a colonnade so skilfully constructed of columns in diminishing sizes that though actually very short it seems to extend quite a distance. The Swedish architect, Nicodemus Tessin, the Younger, in the same way improved the shallow depth of the grounds on which his house in Stockholm is built by erecting at the end of the courtyard a pavilion with a large colonnade at the top which gives sham perspective to the grounds.

It was possible to make a small stage seem large and even to make the flattest wall appear to be a space of great depth by painting pictures on it. But there was one problem which had not yet been solved. When great perspective depth really existed, when there was a great vista, a very deep square, a long street, what could be done to give the observer a feeling of depth as great as it really was? If you look through a colonnade with many hundreds of columns those nearest you will clearly indicate the depth of the foreground but as your eyes travel further along they will quickly reach the point where the perspective diminution is so great that the columns seem to melt into each other and you no longer receive any real impression of depth. To enhance the effect produced by the more distant

*The colonnade around Piazza
di S. Pietro in Rome, erected
1656 — 1663. Designed by Lorenzo Bernini.
See plan p. 54.*

objects they must somehow or other be brought out of line.
Due to the fact that it is curved, the colonnade around the
Piazza di S. Pietro in Rome has a splendour and depth never
found in a straight one. By comparing the large details of the
nearest columns with the more distant, which are drawn into
the field of vision for comparison, it becomes evident that the
piazza is, indeed, a very large one. Standing inside the colonnade, itself, you see the same column steadily repeated at different angles and in varying shades of light until the colonnade
curves away out of sight. During several centuries curved colonnades were a favourite feature of grandiose and extravagant

33

See drawing p. 144.

Landscape etching by Claude Lorrain. In the foreground distinct details in strong dark colours. A road and a bridge lead to the middle ground with the large tree. Behind it the sea and distant mountains.

architecture. They framed the squares in front of palaces. One of the last times the curved colonnade was used in the grand manner was at the beginning of the 19th century when London's shopping district, Regent Street, was built. But even without columns the concave house-row is beautiful because every detail stands out so distinctly. The distant houses, which would be indistinguishable in a straight row, turn more and more toward the observer so that each one is easily perceived.

A broad avenue of trees which cuts a straight path through the landscape has a much more striking effect when it mounts in the distance so that the length of the road becomes more discernible. Strongest of all, however, is the effect produced by terminating the vista with a great monument where the landscape begins to merge into the blue sky. This was understood by Louis XIV's famous landscape gardener, Le Nôtre, who laid out the Champs Elysées as a grand avenue leading from the limits of old Paris to a distant hill. Also Napoleon I realized it when he began the erection of a gigantic triumphal arch on that hill. No real impression of this vast landscape could be obtained if the mile-long avenue did not lead to that clear goal.

Through paintings and theatre decorations the European was taught to look for depth effects in what he saw. Nothing was considered correctly formed or beautiful unless it stood forth distinctly as though on a stage with scenery and set pieces at well-defined distances from the eye. The best results were obtained when the composition could be built up from an ab-

Etched sketch by Claude Lorrain.

34

*Etching with harbour motive
by Claude Lorrain.*

solutely horizontal plane. Harbour paintings with buildings
and long jetties ending in distant towers were popular back-
drops for stage settings; they were also a favourite subject of
the famous French artist, Claude Lorrain (1600-1682), whose
work, more than that of any other painter, determined the
course of European landscape painting over a long period.
Claude Lorrain's landscapes lead the eye into the depth from
one guide-post to another. He knew that it was not enough
to *construct* perspective properly, it must also be properly *accentuated*. Not until then did it become grand perspective.
Over his firm and well-planned compositions he poured his
poetry in the form of classically draped figures, agitated tree-
tops and the golden light of sunsets. At a later date landscape
painters commonly made their pictures even more poetic, more
romantic, by depicting the buildings in ruins half hidden under
wild and luxuriant flora. When Claude Lorrain used trees
in his landscapes they were placed just as deliberately as the
buildings to act as guide-posts to the perspective depth. Often
a single tree stands in the middle ground of the picture to serve
as a measuring rod for the strong perspective diminution of the
background and thereby increases the feeling of spaciousness.
This singly placed tree, "the solitary tree", is found again in
English parks where an attempt has been made to bring Claude
Lorrain's "heroic landscape" to life. These landscaped gardens
were laid out for Englishmen who had learned to appreciate
art and nature on the "grand tour" through France and Italy.

*Etched sketch by Claude Lor-
rain.*

35

Prior Park, near Bath, Eng-land. The park seen from the manor-house.

Just outside the handsome town of Bath in west England there lies an old manor, "Prior Park", set in grounds of unique beauty. If you come there at evening when the sun pours its shimmering golden rays among the trees, you feel as though you had stepped directly into one of Claude Lorrain's landscapes. The park is formed around a long, sloping dale. On the horizon you see the blue hill slopes which surround Bath on all sides. At the bottom of the dale, which lies entirely in shadow, a motionless pond mirrors the light evening sky. Down there stands an artistic covered bridge with Ionic columns supporting the roof, a "Palladian" bridge, just such a piece of architecture as is found in stage settings. Functionally it is meaningless. There is absolutely no need of a bridge there because one can easily go around the pond; and there is even less use for a roof over the bridge and, if one *must* have a roof, it certainly could be raised less expensively than on a whole row of columns. Its mission is exclusively an aesthetic one. It is to produce a picturesque effect with its light arches and columns reflected in the water. Seen from the bottom of the dale it is an effective foreground, a piece of scenery corresponding to the background: the house with its classical portico. And seen from the house it is one of the many perspective guide-posts which emphasize the depth: first the balustrades and vases of the terrace stairway, then the solitary tree, and still further back the columns of the Palladian bridge, finally the border of trees around the park and at the horizon the silhouette of the mountains.

Practically every one of the effects that had been tested in paintings and theatre decorations were carried out in the

*Prior Park, near Bath, Eng-
land. The manor-house seen
from the Palladian bridge.*

great palace grounds, in town-planning and in landscape gardening of the 17th and 18th centuries. It was in keeping with
Absolutism. Perspective is a central projection, that is to say
a form of representation whereby all parts are determined by
their relation to one point, all is centralized. But it was not
Absolutism that created this conception of art. It already existed. Absolutism utilized what it found for its own purposes.
The Middle Ages knew only parallel projection in which
equally large elements are represented equally large. Medieval
towns were conceived in parallel projection, a simple co-ordi-
nation of the elements of the town. This was quite expedient
in colonial cities, new settlements where a certain number
of families were to have equally large houses on sites of equal
size. But Imperial Peking, the capital of autocratic China, was
also planned in parallel projection. No account was taken of
how the whole would look seen from one spot. In Versailles
there was. This is also true of Amaliegade in Copenhagen, the
street in which Harsdorff's colonnade terminates its length,
brings the sidewalks to an end and, at the same time, frames
the view of Saly's fine equestrian statue in the centre of the
spacious Amalienborg Square.

*See drawing page 137 and
140.*

Thus the grand perspective effects were still utilized in
the Neo-Classic architecture at the end of the 18th century.
Indeed, they were not yet forgotten as late as the year 1900.
The French architect, Le Corbusier, who, before all others,
is rightly regarded as the representative of Functionalism,
utilized in his early town-planning projects great symmetrical
axes and even bizarre arches to frame street vistas. But these
projects were not to be characteristic either of him or of the

37

endeavours of modern times. It seems as though the art of painting has exhausted all the possibilities offered by painting in perspective and that now it aims at broadening our comprehension along other lines. It works less with three-dimensional bodies in clearly defined space than with the possibilities of colour on the picture surface itself, within the limits of the frame. From this work completely new ideals have arisen that also affect architecture which now is more spontaneous, working less with the vistas houses can form than with the houses themselves.

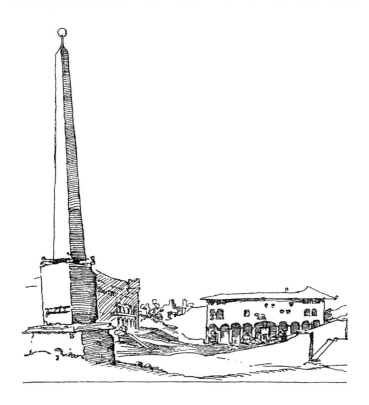

ROME, THE ETERNAL CITY

After spending several days amidst the noise and dirt of the seaport of Naples, it is a relief to come back to Rome. It is like returning home. There is something gentle about the Romans which, I believe, can be found only in a city with a great history, a city that does not live by trade and industry alone. The Romans stand for something of great value, for something indispensable, which gives them dignity and makes it easy for them to be amiable and sympathetic towards others. The inhabitants of Peking are very much the same. They, too, are representatives of an ancient culture.

There were times during the Middle Ages when relics of ancient Rome were destroyed simply because they were pagan. But with the Renaissance came a tremendous enthusiasm for classical art and architecture. Without in any way turning their palaces into museums the Roman aristocracy began collecting antique sculpture. They looked on these ancient statues simply as works of art that would decorate their courtyards and halls. Dilapidated statues were restored to look like new

39

and set up as the owners imagined the artists had intended: between classical columns. The distinctive features of the new stone palaces — vaulted entrance halls, colonnaded courtyards, imposing stone staircases, and regular, high-ceilinged rooms — were carried out with great architectural effect. The Romans did not look for comfort and conveniences in their homes. Such pieces of furniture as armchairs and sofas were entirely unknown. The cool marble of the classical sculpture struck the keynote. The Romans wanted to live in the grand manner of the statuesque figures of the half-visionary architecture of perspective paintings.

The popes realized that by protecting and preserving the antique marbles, by displaying them advantageously, they could give an added nimbus to the holy city. Sixtus IV (1471-1487) began making a collection of antiques on Capitoline Hill. This was done quite independently of the work on the great churches and the papal palaces. Since Antiquity, the Capitol had been the most renowned of the seven famous hills on which Rome was built. The Capitol, which had been the seat of the Roman governing body, the Senate, was the very heart of the city. To restore its eminence would be to underline Rome's illustrious history. Actually, it was not so much the artistic value of the statuary that interested Sixtus IV as the fact that it represented the glory that had been Rome's. After his death other popes continued to add to the collection on the hill. Statues of all kinds were brought there — intimate subjects like the famous Thorn Remover, statues like the two colossal reclining river gods, symbolic works like the bronze she-wolf, supposed to be the very she-wolf that had suckled Romolus and Remus, the founders of Rome. But there was no plan either in the arrangement of the sculpture or in the formation of the hill until Paul III became pope in 1534.

Rome must have been a strange city in those days — large in area within the ancient walls but with few inhabitants, so that many desolate stretches surrounded the few occupied districts. In 1527 Rome had been sacked by Charles de Bourbon. In 1530 it had a population of probably no more than 30,000 within walls built to protect a city of a million. In this vast, almost empty wilderness the effect of the great monuments of Antiquity — the Pantheon, the Colosseum and many

The Colosseum lying among rubble heaps and simple huts at the beginning of the 17th century.

other awe-inspiring ruins, — must have been so much the more overwhelming. Everywhere in the shapeless mounds of earth one stumbled over columns and venerable brickwork from the great and glorious past. Among these pagan ruins later generations had erected the churches that became the goal of pilgrims from all over the Christian world. And now a new monumental city began to rise out of the ruins, a sequel to ancient Rome. In 1506 the foundation stone was laid for the new cathedral of S. Peter which was to replace the medieval one. From now on, plans were laid that would take generations to carry out. The great masters of architecture, Bramante, Raphael, Michelangelo, and the others, waded around in the rubble heaps of Rome and died long before they could see their magnificent projects completed.

During the papacy of Paul III (1534-1549) plans were finally made for the creation of a monumental square on Capitoline Hill. It began, characteristically enough, with the placing of the antique bronze statue of Marcus Aurelius there in 1538. Michelangelo, himself, superintended its erection and he not only designed the pedestal for the statue but also drew the plans for the entire piazza and the buildings that were to frame it. Then, slowly — over a period of several hundred years — his great plan was carried out. The Marcus Aurelius was the only equestrian statue from imperial Rome still in existence. Quite accidentally, or, rather, through an error, it had been preserved. When during the Middle Ages the other statues had been destroyed as pagan, this one had been spared because it was believed to represent the Christian emperor, Constantine the Great. In 1538 its true identity was known but now people were interested in it first and foremost as a great work of art, admired by art lovers, copied by sculptors.

Where the statue stood in ancient Rome is not known. In the Middle Ages it had been placed projecting from a corner of the Lateran, a setting characteristic of the period. At that time sculpture was treated as part of the building and *if* it stood alone, it was placed as though under the protection of the building, close to its walls. With the erection of Marcus Aurelius on Capitoline Hill a new practice was inaugurated. Michelangelo placed the statue so that it would stand in the centre of the new piazza to be laid out there.

*About the Capitol of Rome
see: The Town Planning Review Vol. XII 1927 p. 157
with excellent notes p. 171.*

*See also: Michelangelo Architetto by Armando Schiavo.
Roma 1949, fig. 50 — 76 (with English text).*

*The Capitol piazza during
reconstruction, after a drawing by Heemskerck. In the
middle is seen the Palazzo
del Senatore. Michelangelo's
double stairway is finished
and the equestrian statue in
place. To the right is the
Palace of the Conservatori
before remodelling.*

Old drawings show that the Capitol was just as disorderly
as so many other places in Rome. The famous hill had no form.
It had been plowed up by horsemen and weeds and bushes grew
at random over the uneven terrain. Out of the ruin heaps rose
the old *Palazzo del Senatore,* built over the remains of antique
walls, in the form of a medieval town hall, a robber-baron
stronghold with corner turrets and parapets and a high central
tower. Besides the Senators' Palace there was another official
building, the *Palazzo dei Conservatori,* also quite medieval.
The two buildings were placed so that they formed a rather
sharp angle at one corner.

Out of this picturesque confusion Michelangelo planned to
create rigorous architectonic unity. The irregular hill-top was
to become a platform, a lofty stone-paved terrace approached
by a long flight of stairs. The houses were to be remodelled in
the same spirit. The Senators' Palace which, with its towers
and parapets, produced a decided impression of verticality, was
to be remodelled to form a continuation of the terrace-like composition with a large double staircase leading from the level of
the square up to that of the great hall. There, a powerful string

*Palazzo del Senatore before
remodelling, after an old
drawing. It is seen from the
side. At left, the façade facing the new piazza. The
building is seen with corner
turrets and a high central
tower with loopholes as in a
medieval stronghold.*

course, marking the floor plan on the façade, would produce an
effect of horizontality further accentuated by a great crowning
cornice. Also the central tower would be divided up horizont-
ally and the corner turrets would be taken up in the mass of the
building, losing their independent existence to become, simply,
projecting end bays. The first to be constructed was the imposing outside stairway to the barrel-vaulted hall. Thus, a fitting
background was quickly obtained for the Marcus Aurelius,

*The Capitol piazza during
reconstruction, after a drawing by Heemskerck. At right
Palazzo del Senatore with
Michelangelo's imposing
staircase. In the centre is
seen the great pilgrimage
church, Sta. Maria in Ara-
coeli, which later was hidden by the Capitoline Mu-
seum.*

later (not until about 1600) to include the entire building
which, with its projecting end bays, seems to form a large niche
for the famous equestrian statue. The Conservator's Palace,
to the right of the entrance to the piazza, was also completely
remodelled (finished before Michelangelo's death in 1564).
The twin building to the left, the Capitoline Museum which
houses the Roman antiques, was not finished until 1655.

The design of the piazza indicated a decisive break with
the town-planning ideas of the Renaissance as laid down in the
ideal plans of the theorists. Their piazzi always form regular,
geometric figures: circles, quadrangles, hexagons, octagons,
and they are always designed as independent units, the same
on all sides. The Capitol piazza is a trapezoid, which, however,
is of no great importance in this connection. It became a
trapezoid simply because the walls of the two remodelled buildings formed, as has been noted, a sharp angle at one corner.
But when you stand in it the piazza seems to be rectangular, so
skilfully has the irregularity been counteracted by the pattern
of the pavement — a large oval with lines radiating from the
statue, fashioned of light-coloured stone. No, the crucial difference is that Michelangelo's square is not in itself a handsome,
well-rounded figure but that it consists of a number of
elements, each of which derives its value from its relation to
the rest. Like a stage, the piazza has an opening and a background. There is a crescendo rising from the base of the approach to the top of the Senate tower. Corresponding to this
are the colossal pilasters of the two flanking palaces rising
from the pavement all the way up to the great crowning

43

The bronze statue of the Roman emperor, Marcus Aurelius, the most renowned of all bronzes from Roman Antiquity. 1538 moved to Capitoline Hill to form the centre of the new square to be constructed there.

cornices. The Palace of the Senators has the same pilasters but raised high above the square on the terrace of rusticated masonry of the ground storey.

The man who designed the Capitoline piazza did not conceive his plans as a geometrician but as a sculptor working plastically with his ideas. The piazza has front and back just like the equestrian statue with which it is identified. The buildings are akin to the sculpture which so admirably unites tenseness with statuesque calm. Every nerve in the horse seems to quiver while a feeling of peace emanates from the rider — not only from the hand extended as if in benediction, but from his entire being. It was with deliberate intention that the unknown sculptor gave the horse's mighty trunk its plain full-bodied forms which seem even more massive and simple compared to the small head and slender legs with their strongly accentuated details. The ears, eyes and nostrils are holes deeply cut in the bronze. The veins and folds of skin are moulded like refined ornaments. Also the rider's head is small, with hair and beard carried out in a delicate, decorative style. The hands and feet are as elegant in form as the whole is simple and striking. The rider has his own character yet sculpturally is one with the horse. His thighs clasp the broad flanks while his legs and feet stand out, free and vital. This statue is not a collection of beautiful details and even less a naturalistic reproduction of a man on horseback. It is a concentrated and expressive composition in which each element has meaning only in its relation to the whole.

Michelangelo worked with the same problems as the sculptor of antiquity who modelled Marcus Aurelius, not only in his sculpture but also in his architecture. In profile the equestrian statue is seen against a building with the same character of large, pure planes (in pilasters and walls) emphasized by strongly marked details with deep shadows. The entire façade is formed like the partition between the nave and a side aisle of a church. The *nave,* the large room, is the piazza itself, and corresponding with it on the façade are the *tall* Corinthian pilasters. The side aisle is a shady colonnade along the ground storey of the building and related to it are *small* Ionic columns. Thus, the piazza merges into the palace and the colonnaded house emerges onto the square. The building seems vast with

*The statue of Marcus Au-
relius on the base designed
by Michelangelo seen against
the Capitoline Museum which
was carried out according to
plans drawn by the great
architect but not finished until 100 years after his death.*

its colossal pilasters which appear even greater than they are
in comparison to the small columns and their details,
which display the same mannerisms as those of the horse.
It was against all the architectural theory of the Renaissance to use columns and pilasters of varying scales on the same
façade. It seemed a *baroque* idea. But for Michelangelo it was
a step in the right direction away from the sterile text-book
architecture which lacked vitality. He worked deliberately
with these contrasts of scales, of solids and voids, of architecturally determined space that merged into the solid building
and bodies that emerged into the space. The word "baroque",
as applied to architecture, is no longer a disparaging one.
It is the name given to that vigorous architectural style
which, in Michelangelo's spirit but almost a hundred years
after him, was to leave its stamp on Rome. The masters
of Baroque did not intend their art as a departure from
the style of Antiquity. In Rome they felt, and justifiedly so,
that they were carrying on in the same spirit. They wished to
create a Rome that would be a worthy successor to the Rome
the ruins spoke of — and they succeeded. In other countries
Baroque monument squares are usually built round a king's
statue. It is said they were created to glorify the monarchy.
But this first monument square does not glorify the pope who
had it built. It is, if anything is, art for art's own sake. The

45

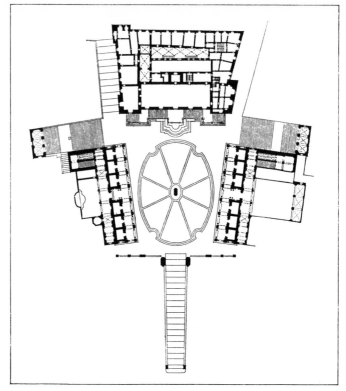

Plan of Rome's Capitol, scale 1 : 2000. Below, the great ramp leading up to the piazza. At right, the Palace of the Conservatori, at left, the Capitoline Museum. Back centre, Palazzo del Senatore.

dishevelled hill, the Capitol, has been conquered. Not in the sense of levelling its steep gradients. On the contrary, they were given form, transformed into an imposing flight of stairs, magnificent as cascades. The horizontal planes have been emphasized, the hill divided into mounting levels and made even higher by the buildings so that it seems to draw itself up proudly before your eyes. It has been made a monument to Rome, itself, the city that was once the mighty heart of a world empire and later the mother of the holy Roman church, the centre of learning and art.

The new Capitol won admiration and fame. Engravers spread views of it all over the world. But it cannot be seen in one picture. It is necessary to stroll about on it, to experience ascending the ramp, *la Cordonata,* to the summit where serene peace reigns. It is only a small square, small enough to be completely dominated by the equestrian statue on its low base. From the colonnades one should wander into the courtyards of the palaces, where the same dimensions are repeated, into the buildings where the antique sculpture is set up.

46

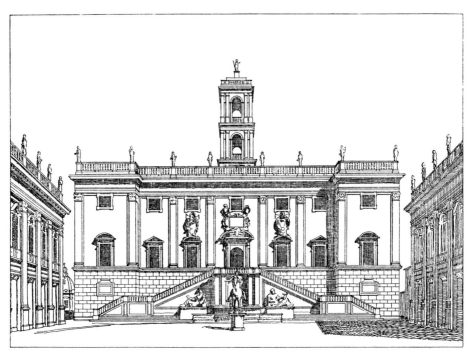

Capitol Square in Rome. Centre, Palazzo del Senatore, at right, The Palace of the Conservatori, at left, Capitoline Museum.

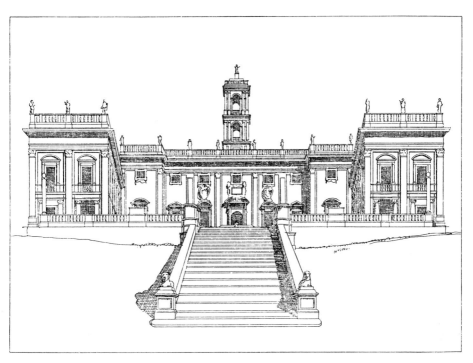

Capitol Square in Rome, seen from foot of the ramp leading up to piazza.

47

More than a hundred years before the introduction of the absolute monarchy in France an artist conceived this square, conceived an artistic form which seemingly was created for the glorification of kings.

With the grand perspective and with Baroque architecture — two things closely related — *motifs* were given which the absolute monarchy could use, and which, today, seem inseparably bound up with Absolutism.

Rome was not satisfied with this one great monument. An effort was made to draw great lines through the whole vast city by laying out a new network of streets. Sixtus V was pope for only five years, from 1585 to 1590, but in that short time he accomplished wonders. He not only busied himself with foreign politics and brought order in the finances, but he also finished the dome of S. Peter's, gave the city decent drinking water, and marked out the main points of the great network of streets he had planned. This remarkable man, who had begun life as a poor country lad, a shepherd boy, was to do more for the great city of Rome than anyone else. His name figures in all the great plans that were to change the face of the city. That this was at all possible is undoubtedly due to the fact that much of this work had been prepared before he became pope and much of it was continued after his death.

The matter of the drinking water was a very important one. In ancient times the city had been well supplied with pure cold water that was brought to Rome from the mountains through a dozen aqueducts. But these were now in ruins and the Romans were forced to drink the much less palatable water of the Tiber. In 1570 one of the ancient aqueducts had been repaired. Under Sixtus V another was put in order and in 1611 a third was made to function again. Once more Rome had pure water. This was not only a sanitary improvement. It resulted in such an abundance of sparkling spring water that it could be used for fountains and rippling cascades all over the sun-parched city. The water from Sixtus V's aqueduct, Acqua Felice, fed the magnificent fountain, Fontanone dell'Acqua Felice. (The original name of Sixtus V was Felice Peretti.)

Every square received its fountain, and through the centuries artists created new variations of the same theme: rippling, splashing water, whether jetting forth from sculptured groups

set up amidst the columns of the many decorative façades or from single fountains, embellished with tritons and river gods, standing in the centres of squares. The sound of hundreds of playing fountains became the melody of Rome, faintly audible behind the loud noise of the city by day, clearly heard at night when the great metropolis lay in hushed tranquillity.

Though Sixtus V did not live long enough actually to build the great new thoroughfares that were to change Rome from a small medieval town with a maze of streets to a city of great vistas, he at any rate clearly marked out where they were to start and where they were to end. He did this with obelisks and columns. The *obelisk*, the tall, slender, almost square stone pillar, slightly tapering toward the top and terminated by a pyramidion, originated in Egypt and, in Rome's case, actually came from there. The Egyptian obelisk (the tallest known is 105 feet high) is a monolith, a finely polished stone column hewn out of a single block; standing upright it is a phallus, in ancient times worshipped in Egypt as a symbol of the generative power of nature.

When the ancient Romans came to Egypt they admired the obelisks so much that they felt they could not go home without them. As early as the year 10, the Emperor Augustus had an obelisk brought to Rome as a symbol of the subjection of Egypt. It now stands in the Piazza del Popolo. How they were able, with the transport facilities of those days, to send obelisks from Egypt to Rome is a mystery. The largest of them weighed 430 tons. But however it was done, there are now twelve of them in the Eternal City.

Just as the antique Marcus Aurelius statue had been used for the focal-point of the Capitol piazza, the Baroque architects now used the ancient obelisks they found lying about Rome, raising them at points they particularly wished to identify. In this way the obelisks became gigantic surveyor's rods marking out a system of straight lines, the plan of the future. For the Egyptians they had been part of a religious cult, for the ancient Romans a symbol of world dominion, but for the popes and their architects they had no symbolic meaning whatsoever, only an artistic one. They gave character to the city and its squares, stood as guide-posts for the new, straight streets that were to be laid out over hill and dale.

See : How Pope Sixtus V lost a Road, by J. A. F. Orbaan. The Town Planning Review, Vol. XIII p. 121 and p. 257.

The two domed churches from the end of the 17th century which face Piazza del Popolo. Seen from the Piazza facing south. Between them Via Flaminia, Rome's Corso.

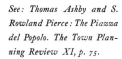

See: Thomas Ashby and S. Rowland Pierce: The Piazza del Popolo. The Town Planning Review XI, p. 75.

The main gateway to Rome was the Porta del Popolo entrance. Just inside it Sixtus V had a great obelisk erected in 1589 as the starting point of four new avenues. The most easterly, however, was given up as it proved impossible to carry it over the steep mountain-sides of Monte Pincio. Remaining were the three others: the one in the middle, Via Flaminia, which leads directly into the heart of Rome; the western thoroughfare, Via Ripetta, skirting the Tiber; and the eastern, Via Babuino, adjoining the slopes of Monte Pincio. Via Ripetta led to a ferry crossing where an architectural arrangement of terraces and stairs led down to the river. A twin staircase, the still-existent "Spanish Stairway" with its 137 steps, led up to the top of the hill. Here, in front of a church, a new obelisk was erected to mark the starting point of a new thoroughfare, Via Sistina, which Sixtus V planned to run directly southeast to an obelisk raised in 1587 behind the large church of Santa Maria Maggiore. From this church another rectilineal street led to the Church of the Lateran at the southeastern boundary of the city wall, where the world's largest obelisk was erected in 1588.

Immediately on passing through Porta del Popolo the visitor enters a square, Piazza del Popolo. Today it is an oval but at that time it was a long, narrow trapezoid converging towards the gateway and with long garden walls on either side. Facing the city, one saw the three thoroughfares thrusting deep into the town. The two triangular building sites form an effective front with two symmetrical domed churches strongly emphasizing the solid mass of the houses advancing toward the open space of the piazza.

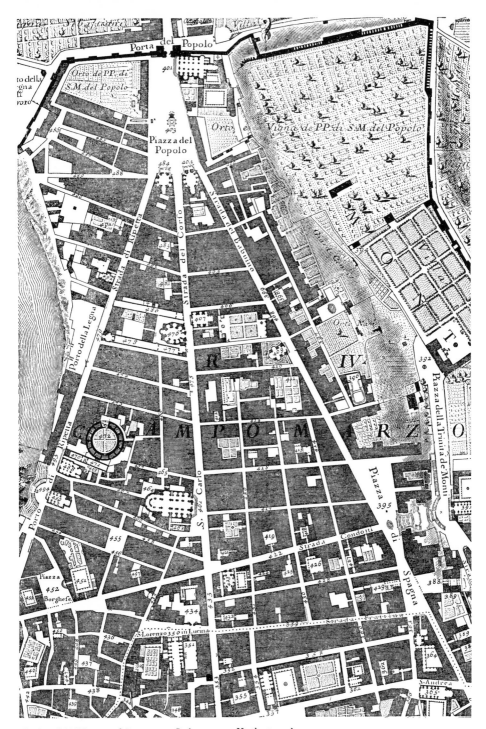

Section of Nolli's map of Rome, 1748. Scale 1 : 6000. North upward.

599 *Sta. Maria della Pace* ➤

605 *Piazza Navona with
three fountains* ➤

837 *The antique domed Pantheon. Building's interior just
as large as the square in
front of it.* ➤

771 *Typical horseshoe-formed
Baroque theatre.* ➤

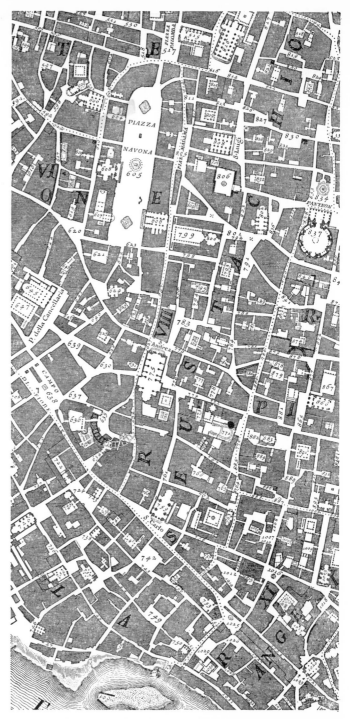

Section of Nolli's map of Rome, 1748. Scale 1 : 6000.

The three avenues are like narrow clefts in the densely built city. The map from the Baroque period gives a vivid impression of the whole situation. The street blocks, faced with houses, are finely hatched. The hollowed-out spaces in the dark tone indicate the many delightful surprises to be found in Rome. There are church interiors with many chapels. Through a murky church entrance, which is always open, you plunge into the vast, vaulted interior where light filters down from cupolas high overhead. Other churches are round or oval, wreathed with altar niches. Often the church interior is larger than the narrow street you have just left. Sometimes the doorways take you through the solid mass of the palaces into light, colonnaded courtyards. It is difficult to think of these palaces as homes, difficult to imagine an everyday existence in such monumental surroundings. And as a matter of fact the inhabitants were seldom at home and guests were almost never received in the palaces. The aristocracy met in the afternoon, between five and seven o'clock, in their splendid coaches on the main thoroughfare of Rome, the middle of the three new roads running from Piazza del Popolo, Via Flaminia. The magnificently painted and gilded coaches rolled slowly up, after the heat of the day, when the narrow street lay in shadow. There the *signori* stepped out, to take the air, as we say. There was probably not very much fresh air to be had in that narrow street but that gave them so much the more time for visiting. The ladies remained in the upholstered carriages while the gentlemen went calling from one to the other. This was called driving *Corso,* which is the same word as the English "course". From this custom Rome's main thoroughfare has come to be called, simply, the Corso. This was the prelude to the evening's entertainment, the opera, where again the ladies remained seated — this time in their newly upholstered boxes lining the horseshoe interior — receiving callers and — when the spirit moved them — listening to the singing or music for a change.

The streets were like corridors through Rome's great building, the open squares were reception halls of the most varying shapes. There was the long Piazza Navona, built over the walls of an ancient race track. The piazza had three large fountains and the entire pavement could be flooded by plugging the drains so that it became an enormous pond in which

About the piazzas see: The Town Planning Review Vol. XII p. 57.

*The church of Sta. Maria
della Pace in Rome. Façade
by Pietro da Cortona, 1656.*

churches and palaces were mirrored while the aristocracy
amused itself driving Corso through the pond mirror and the
pedestrians stood, dry-shod, on the sidewalks watching the fun.
A narrow street runs from this large piazza to the quaint
square dominated by the church of Santa Maria della Pace.

The greatest of all the monuments of the Baroque period
is S. Peter's and its magnificent piazza. The domed cathedral
which was to replace the medieval basilican church was originally planned as a central building symmetrically arranged
on two axial lines but later the interior was lengthened toward
the east with a façade added across the front and, later still,
the noble entrance piazza was laid out in front of that, again.
Also in this case the work on the piazza began with the erection
of an enormous obelisk to mark the centre. It was again
Sixtus V who had it raised here in 1586. The piazza did not
receive its present form until 70 years later. It was designed by
Bernini and though it clearly defines an architectural space
it does not enclose it. The imposing colonnades both separate
and join the city and the piazza.

Such was the Rome of the pope, the nobility, and the people.
The city where both the great and the lowly knew how to live
in harmony, where at carnival time there was neither rank nor
class, where great artists formed the city and the inhabitants,
themselves, were artists enough to know how to live in it.

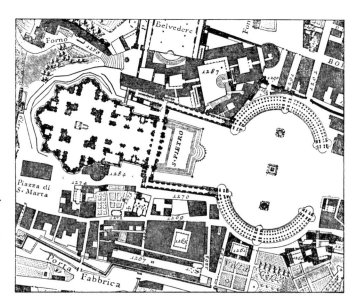

*Section of Nolli's map of
Rome, 1748, showing S. Peter's church and square with
Bernini's colonnades. — Compare illustration p. 33.*

Part of a view of Paris at the time of the Musketeers, from an engraving by Israel Silvestre. Right bank of Seine looking toward Pont Neuf and Place Dauphine. In the background are seen the gables and spires of gothic Paris.

THE PARIS OF THE MUSKETEERS

During the reigns of Louis XIII and Louis XIV there lived in Paris a captain of musketeers called d'Artagnan. His life was full of romantic adventure, and it was not long before writers became aware of it. Already at the beginning of the 17th century a book was published purporting to be his memoirs — personal reminiscences, both authentic and fictional, were very popular at the time. It was this book "d'Artagnan's Memoirs", that inspired Alexandre Dumas to write his immortal trilogy: "The Three Musketeers", "Twenty Years After", and "The Viscount de Bragelonne". All three should be read and preferably in succession. The last two are by no means the usual attempt to reap the rewards of a best-seller by rehashing the same ingredients over and over again. On the contrary, all three vary greatly and the third, which was Robert Louis Stevenson's favourite book, is probably the wittiest. They unfold a series of amazing episodes that take place during three important periods of the history of Paris and France and are just as different from each other as these three epochs were. It is true that the complicated intrigues are Dumas' own inventions and the main characters, the musket-

A musketeer, after a contemporary etching by Jacques Callot.

55

eers, his brain-children in everything but name. But they are
not only stirring "cloak and sword" dramas. The important
political events which form the ever-changing background of
the adventures of the musketeers are skilfully worked up from
sound historical sources which Dumas' collaborator, Maquet,
was so expert at digging out of libraries and archives.

The first and most famous of the books, "The Three
Musketeers", begins in 1625. From Gascogny the penniless
young d'Artagnan comes to the capital. With him we enter
the Paris of Cardinal Richelieu, a noisy, adventurous town
full of intrigue and youthful rivalry which is always settled
by duels. It is the struggle of all against all — we are still
in the Middle Ages when knightly sports were cultivated. It
is a story of courage and *armes blanches*.

This use of sharp weapons, which we continually meet in
the book, is in keeping with a needle-pointed sharpness in the
silhouette of Paris, formed by the towers and spires and lofty
gables of its buildings. When the great Italian architect, Bernini, came to France forty years later, bringing with him
memories of the domes and long, horizontal cornices of the
papal city, he said with contempt that Paris looked like a collection of chimneys and that the whole city resembled the spiked
instrument for carding wool. It was an exceedingly congested
town with narrow, crooked streets, high gabled houses, and
Gothic churches. And it was not only the street view and the
city silhouette that were characterized by building after building thrusting heavenward with pointed gables and spires. Even
the palaces consisted of a number of individual buildings facing
each other with steep, hipped roofs.

In 1564 Catherine de Medici, the widow of Henri II
(1547-49), commenced the building of a palace, the Tuileries,
which was to be an important link in the development of Paris.
It burst the bounds of the all too cramped city because the
queen desired a large, rectangular garden in connection with
it. Therefore it was laid beyond the city walls, an amazing
structure, quite exotic with its wealth of domes and spires, as
Merian's engraving shows. Three years later the queen built
a 1570-foot gallery along the Seine which connnected the
old, almost Gothic Louvre, inside the walls, with the new
Tuileries, outside, and made a magnificent setting for the

*Lorenzo Bernini, who de-
signed the Entrance piazza
of S. Peter's in Rome, 1656—
63, (see pp. 33 and 54) was
called to Paris in 1665 to
draw plans for the new
Louvre.*

*Entrance to Place Dauphine
with houses from the time of
Henri IV. Place Dauphine
can be seen on the map at
the bottom of p. 59 and in the
views on pages 57 and 61.*

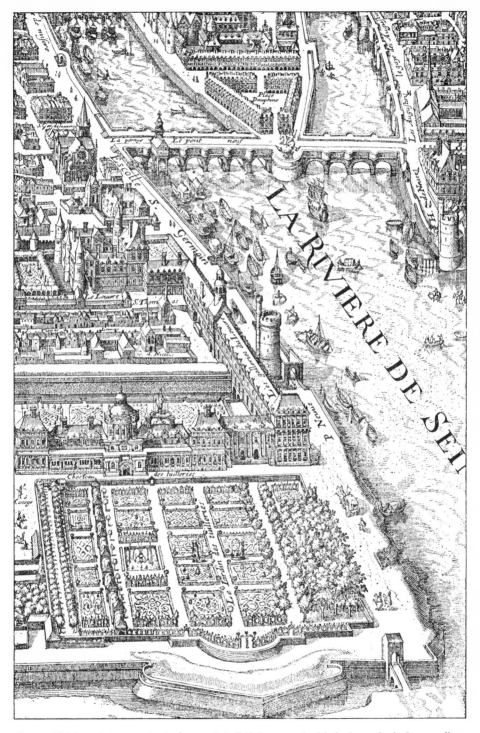

Section of Merian's Paris, 1615. In the foreground the Tuileries connected with the Louvre by the Louvre gallery.

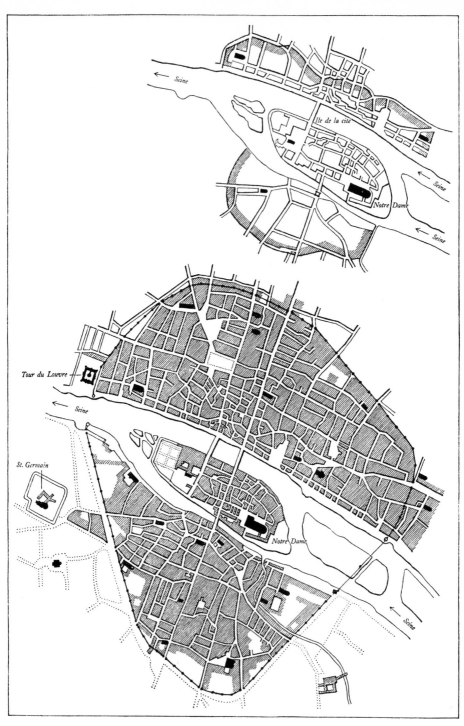

Above, Paris in early Middle Ages; below, Paris 1180—1225. Both maps: Scale 1 : 20.000. North upward.

58

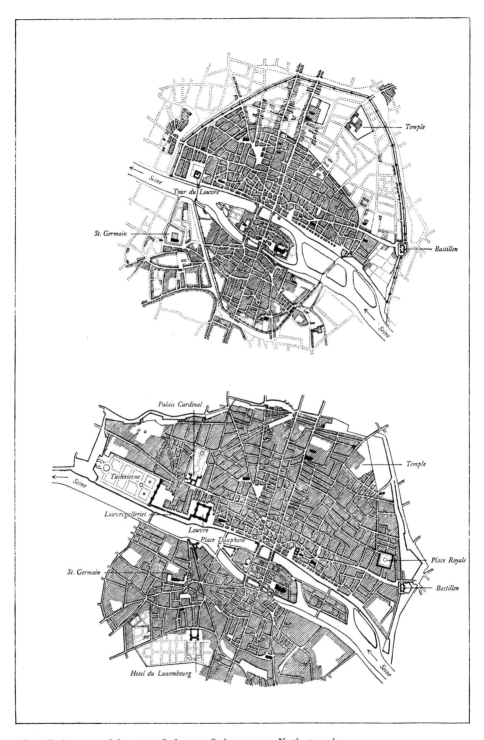

Above, Paris, c. 1370; below, 1676. Both maps: Scale 1 : 40.000. North upward.

59

Place Royale (now Place des Vosges) at the time of Louis XIII with equestrian statue of King, after engraving by Israel Silvestre.

On the maps, pp. 58 and 59 the old castle of the Louvre can be seen at top left. On the earliest map it lies outside of the city, like an outpost; later it is protected by walls and connected with the Tuileries by the Louvre gallery.

river, itself. Inside the city, the gabled houses crowded out onto the very bridges where they stood in compact rows. But Henri IV built a bridge, *Pont Neuf* (opened to traffic in 1606), which was exempt from building so that the river and the Louvre gallery could be seen from it. Pont Neuf united the two banks of the Seine with the prow-like end of the island in its middle, la Cité, where the king laid out the Place Dauphine, in honour of his son, the Dauphin (later Louis XIII). It was open toward the bridge but otherwise entirely surrounded by houses of a uniform style. Despite all effort to give this new square classic unity, it, too, seemed almost Gothic with the emphasis on verticality that was produced by tall windows, quoins at the corners, high dormers with stone fronts rising above the cornice, and lofty chimneys crowning the steep roofs.

Also in the eastern part of the city an attempt was made to create greater unity. Earlier, a tournament field had lain there, la Tournelle, where Henri II received the wound from which he died. On this site Henri IV planned a large square, The Place Royale, which was first completed after his death. It was a quadrangle, completely enclosed by a border of stately houses, all of the same design. Until now the nobility had lived in country chateaux or in "hotels" in various parts of the city. The Place Royale can be regarded as a visible effort to bring the aristocracy under the control of an integrating idea, that of forming a background for the monarchy. Instead of a galaxy of petty princes, opposing each other and the king, they were

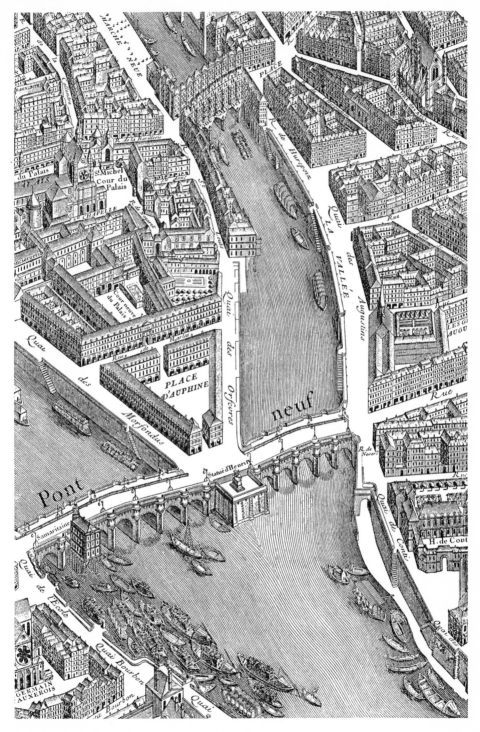

Section of Turgot's plan of Paris, 1731, showing Pont Neuf and Place Dauphine.

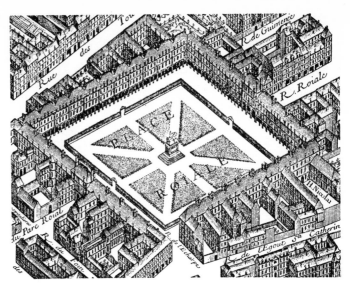

*Place Royale (now Place des
Vosges), from Turgot's plan.*

now to become a part of the great pageantry of the court. The
Place Royale was framed by 38 uniform houses of red brick
and stone quoins with windows in rows of four symmetrically
arranged on the façades, surmounted by lofty dormers. In the
centre of the north and south rows a taller building was inserted containing a gateway entrance to the square. Later,
streets were broken through at two of the corners. The houses
were united on the ground level by an arcade but at the top
they were separated with the sides of the steep hipped roofs
facing each other. Henri IV had planned the square for cosmopolitan living in the otherwise cramped city. As in earlier days
the place was again the scene of tournaments and jousting, for
example on the occasion of the marriage of Louis XIII in
1615. In 1639 it became a great monument square when
Richelieu erected a statue of Louis XIII in its centre and later
again it was turned into a garden — today a most drab garden
in a slum area.

Like Henri II, Henri IV married an Italian and a daught-
er of the Medicis: Marie de Medici. After her husband's
death she built a palace for herself, the Palais de Luxembourg, and it, too, was placed just outside the city limits where
there was room for a large park. Far from the heart of the
town, d'Artagnan found it a place most suitable for duelling.
The Luxembourg is typical of many French palaces of the
period, composed of a number of units built round a court:

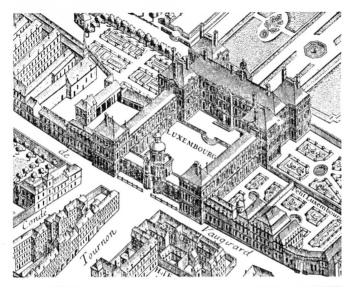

*Palais de Luxemborg, from
Turgot's plan.*

a three-storeyed "corps de logis", corner pavilions with pyramid roofs, side wings, and a domed entrance building. Only
one person in all France could compete with royalty in building activities: Cardinal Richelieu. He worked unceasingly
to make the power of the king — and with it his own —
absolute. In Paris he built the great Palais Cardinal (now
Palais Royal) which, like the palaces of the two dowager
queens, had a large, rectangular park thrusting out over the
city limits. In the 18th century, long after the boundaries had
been extended beyond it, the park was remodelled into an
arcaded square surrounded by buildings.

"Twenty Years After" takes place during a dramatic period
in the history of Paris. Richelieu is dead. The musketeers judge
him now quite differently; formerly their enemy, he now becomes the great cardinal and his epoch a time of grandeur and
adventure. While he lived his strong will had held all the
mutually antagonistic powers in check, but now they break
loose. In 1648 the Fronde revolt begins, cunningly made to
appear an uprising of the people but proving more and more
to be the last stand of the aristocracy against the king and the
threatening absolutism. The densely populated city with its
narrow, crooked streets and large proletariat was as if made
for revolution. The Queen Mother, Anne of Austria, was
forced to flee with the young king to safety. Though the monarchy triumphed in the end, Louis XIV never forgot the

63

humiliations he suffered under the Fronde and the thought of living in Paris was repugnant to him. From the French capital the reader follows the musketeers to London where another revolution is under way, a revolution that was to end quite differently than that in Paris: with the dethronement and execution of Charles I. It was looked upon as the final victory of Parliament and the City over the monarchy, a decisive factor in the development of London as a free commercial town.

In the last of the volumes about the musketeers, ten years after the foregoing, we see the triumph of Absolutism under Louis XIV. Porthos goes to court where he has an eating match with the great king, great also in appetite! Where the first volume treats of fighting with keen-edged swords, the last describes an unending round of love affairs, intrigue, and festivities, at a court where duelling is banned. Absolutism was outwardly manifested by the removal of the court from the congested, seething city to the open country of Versailles, where, little by little, a small hunting chateau was transformed into an amazing palace over a quarter of a mile long with hundreds of rooms, all housed under one low roof and with all façades united by one crowning cornice. As a sort of adjunct to the palace a town was built nearby with three long avenues all focused on the same spot: the centre of the palace. The town is an appendage to the court, just as necessary as kitchen and pantry are to a dining-room. The palace façade faces the park which is a vast landscape accentuated architecturally in deep perspective from the terrace to the horizon.

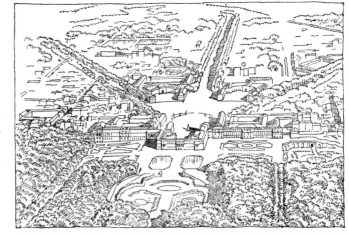

Versailles seen from the air. In the foreground the park with the 400 meter long palace front. Behind the palace the city with the three main thoroughfares bordered with trees which are all focused on the equestrian statue of Louis XIV in the courtyard of the palace.

Raphael: "The School of
Athens", fresco painting,
the Vatican, Rome.

THE VILLA

The Italian villa of the Renaissance or Baroque period was
an entirely different type of building from that which we
know today. It represented a particular way of life, certain high
ideals which Raphael has described in his famous painting, the
so-called "School of Athens". It does not depict a school at all,
in any ordinary sense of the word, but is, rather, a glorification
of Grecian culture. Raphael desired to give, in a single painting,
an impression of the group of Greek thinkers whom the Renaissance admired and cultivated.

As the central figures, around whom all the others are
gathered, we see Plato and Aristotle. Plato is pictured as a
venerable greybeard, monumental in his dignity and in his
extreme verticality in the composition. At his side stands Aristotle, turning toward him, gesticulating, so that his robe bill-
ows about him in great folds. Around these central figures,
which in their lively contrast form such a powerful focal-point,
are a multitude of persons. Each one is a distinct personality,
but a flowing movement from the one to the other unites them
in a great *ensemble*. Socrates is easily recognized and tradition singles out a number of other historical personages: Dio-
genes, Heraclitus, Archimedes, Pythagoras, and many others.
It is a brilliant academy of intellect and learning, given life
by Raphael's genius. Several of the figures have the monumental balance of Plato in the centre of the picture, others display
the same lively animation as Aristotle.

65

But common to them all is a harmonious plasticity only found in those who have perfect control over their bodies. That it was possible for Raphael, in the Vatican, in the papal palace itself, to glorify Greek *intellectual* life by depicting athletically developed *bodies,* was due to the fact that he was giving expression to an aesthetic ideal. That which was new in this glorification of the great men of philosophy, arithmetic and geometry as harmonious human-beings, is best understood when we recall the ideals of the Middle Ages. Then, too, there were philosophers who were admired. But they were the holy men of the church. The ideal was the ascetic, almost disembodied thinker, who lived in mystical rapport with a supernatural world and endowed mankind with profound meditations on the life to come. And, for that matter, the Middle Ages also had its hero. He was the knight in armour, burdened with weapons — and with ritual no less rigid than that of the church. Raphael's figures are the result of an enamoured study of the human body, itself, and in contrast to both saint and knight they denote the liberation of spirit and body. The harmonious individual, who moves about unhampered, in light, classical robes or entirely naked, was his ideal. The holy men of the Middle Ages had been pictured meditating in quiet rooms, secluded from the tempestuous outside world behind thick walls. These rooms could be very pleasant with their painted wooden ceilings, their deep recessed windows with leaded panes, their oak work tables and many homely touches. But Raphael's ideal beings, who concerned themselves with the living world, with space, astronomy, geometry, did not belong in monkish cells. Their personalities craved high-ceilinged, spacious chambers in keeping with the sublimity of their minds. Raphael's ideal beings move about at ease in a noble, classic architecture; a great barrel-vaulted corridor leads to a circular central hall and on through new triumphal arches in the distant background into nature's room under the blue skies of the south. The foreground widens out to a terrace with steps leading down to a level pavement tiled in a large, clear design. This is no impregnable sanctuary which shuts out life; these men are in direct contact with the world and look on the architecture simply as a framework, just as the great ruins of Antiquity now appeared to the modern Roman.

It would be quite impossible to realize such an architectural
vision in a city. Even in the Rome of that day which, as already
mentioned, was widespread with few inhabitants, a building
that was open to its surroundings would only draw narrow
streets and dilapidated houses into its orbit. But the wealthy
noble families who had their palaces in town also had country
places in the mountains where there was ample space and
magnificent views. It had been the custom to build them as
regular strongholds, with heavy corner turrets. But now defensive considerations were no longer taken into account
(though the period was by no means a peaceful one), and new
house types were created in which the projecting corner structures were connected by loggias. Soon the loggia became of
first importance. This cool, colonnaded gallery, which formed
a lovely link between the sun-dappled garden and the rooms
inside, was the very feature that made the building a villa,
that is to say a dwelling attractively combining indoors and
out. From the road side you entered a cool, grotto-like vesti-
bule which led to the large, airy, central chamber that again
opened on the loggia toward the garden where the axial lines
of the building continued in an architectonic landscape of
terraces with stairways, fountains and cascades. You could sit
indoors and hear coolness, itself, rippling down among the ever-
greens. The palaces in Rome were huge, closed blocks facing
the streets in dignified aloofness. Certain of the villas, too, like
the famous Villa d'Este in Tivoli, rose up sheer from the side
of the mountains, a solid background for the garden, the only
villa-like feature being a projecting loggia. But most of the
villas were richer in architectural design with wings projecting
from the main block, with openings in the form of loggias and
with an extra storey and balcony added for better enjoyment
of the fine view.

The villas in the mountains around Rome became famous
but those near the little provincial town of Vicenza, in the
Republic of Venice, designed by Andrea Palladio, were even
more admired. He united Venetian traditions with the classic
ideals of the day. A wealthy art patron, himself a classical
scholar, helped Palladio to go to Rome, and repeated journeys
to the many antique ruins determined his whole conception of
architecture.

Villa d'Este in Tivoli near Rome, seen from the garden.

67

Andrea Palladio: Villa Pio-vene, Lonedo. Approach stairway.

The wealthy villa dweller, as depicted by Paolo Vero-nese in a painting at Villa Maser, near Vicenza, built by Palladio.

Palladio wanted to create a reality that would correspond to the ideal Raphael had evoked in his painting of ancient Greece. A modern person thinks of moving to the country as an escape from the cosmopolitan life of the city to a more primitive existence. But in Palladio's day just the opposite was true. Life in a little, walled town like Vicenza was the primitive one, cramped and dirty and with small opportunity for magnificent display. To be able to realize what was then considered a civilized life it was absolutely necessary to live in the country. There it was possible to build according to the ideals of the time. There you could live a life of beauty and of the spirit. A villa was a great establishment with space for many people, a whole colony in itself. It had a large domestic staff, its own farm which could keep the great house supplied with fresh country products, and it had rooms for many guests so that out there, far from the common herd of the town, the owner could always surround himself with a gathering of choice spirits.

The Venetian noblemen were very wealthy and knew how to live in great style. Because of her geographical position midway between East and West, Venice saw all the luxury of the Orient pass through her harbours on its way to western Europe. This left its stamp on the city, on its buildings, and on all its colourful life. Venetian architecture was in many ways reminiscent of both Byzantine and Moorish art. Each palace had its loggia out toward the canal, often with pointed arches, more Arabian than Gothic. Such a loggia was not high and airy like that of a Roman villa. Rather, it was like a room with one wall closely lined with window openings carried out in a lacework of stone. In contrast to it, the other rooms of the palace were poorly supplied with windows. In every one of the large chambers there were usually only two windows in its entire length, one at each end, so that a strong light fell on the end walls, which is flattering to paintings and sculpture, while the centre of the room lay in shadow, protected from the hot rays of the southern sun. On the exterior this gave a special character to the façade. There seemed to be a desire to emphasize the breadth of the building by placing the windows as far apart as possible. Ordinary small houses in Vicenza, which stand in rows along the streets and are only one room wide, usually have two windows to each storey, spaced in the same manner, one at each corner. The wide overhanging eaves were designed as a protection, not only from the sun but from the rain.

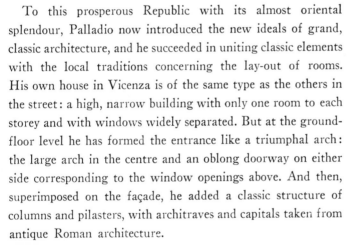

Palladio's house in Vicenza.

To this prosperous Republic with its almost oriental splendour, Palladio now introduced the new ideals of grand, classic architecture, and he succeeded in uniting classic elements with the local traditions concerning the lay-out of rooms. His own house in Vicenza is of the same type as the others in the street: a high, narrow building with only one room to each storey and with windows widely separated. But at the ground-floor level he has formed the entrance like a triumphal arch: the large arch in the centre and an oblong doorway on either side corresponding to the window openings above. And then, superimposed on the façade, he added a classic structure of columns and pilasters, with architraves and capitals taken from antique Roman architecture.

Paolo Veronese: The feast of St. Gregory. Painting at Monte Berico. Vicenza.

69

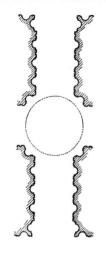

Plan of rooms depicted in
"The School of Athens" —
Scale: 1 : 500.

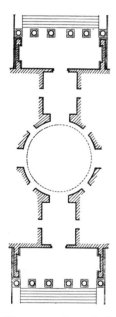

The sequence of rooms in the
Villa Rotunda from one loggia to the other. — Scale:
1 : 500.

70

The Venetian palaces possessed all possible grandeur, expensive materials and glowing colours. Space, alone, had to be used with great economy. It was not easy for the architect to produce his effects by arranging the rooms in architecturally planned relation to each other. In most of the palaces he was satisfied if only he could find space enough for the necessary number of rooms and succeed in placing the principal chambers out toward the canal. The entrance had to be on the same side as the loggia, the offices and servants' quarters could not be entirely segregated from the drawing-rooms. The canals were the brilliant scenes of gondola regattas, and the houses were to be looked on as stage boxes where people could sit, beautifully costumed, watching the performances.

In the country, where there was ample space, all this was quite different. Palladio's villas are sumptuous, but it is not material and colour that have been used so lavishly, it is space. There is much room in them, and great effects have been obtained by the manner in which the regular rooms have been arranged in relation to each other. Instead of colourfully decorated ceilings there are plastered barrel-vaults and cupolas. The loggia has become an entire hall with great, classical columns. Often it is like a smaller building projecting from the main block. From this broad loggia you enter a narrow *salle*. (See Villa Piovene page 73). Most famous of all the villas was the so-called Villa Rotunda, an almost square block with a large, colonnaded portico on all four sides. Ascending the broad flight of stairs to one of the porticoes you are aware of the same composition of rooms as in the "School of Athens". From the broad, open portico you enter the barrel-vaulted hall which leads you into the circular domed chamber in the centre. From there the axial line continues through a new barrel-vaulted hall out to the portico on the other side. In Raphael's painting the architecture seems immense. It is like a great church. Actually it is not a huge edifice he has depicted; it is no larger than Villa Rotonda where almost the same sequence of noble rooms is found. The difference between the architecture of the painting and that of the actual building is that in the former you see it all at one glance while in Palladio's house you have a view of only one room at a time, as you pass from door to door.

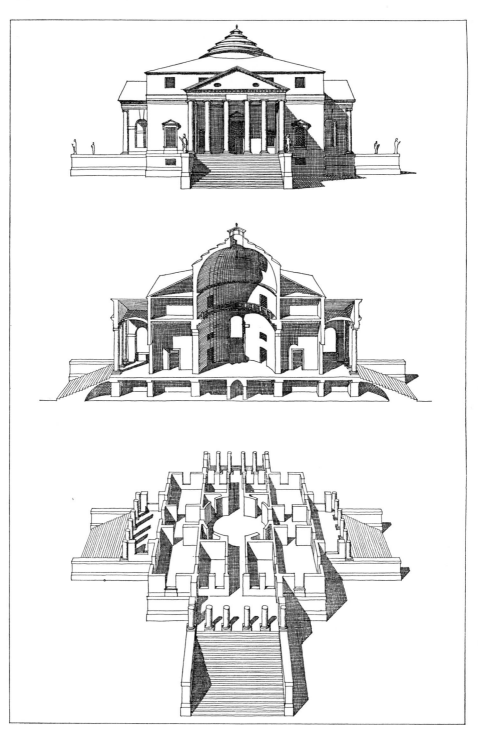

Andrea Palladio: Villa Rotunda, Vicenza. — Sectional drawing scaled to 1 : 500.

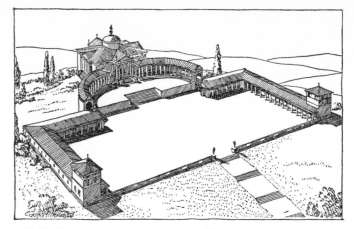

Andrea Palladio: Villa Tri-sino, Meledo. Bird's-eye-view.

Palladio designed another villa (Trisino) on similar lines with two axes that cross each other at right angles in a large, circular, domed hall. In this villa he has added a lower colonnaded wing which frames the entrance in a large arch, a *motif* which was, later, often to be repeated in European architecture.

See drawing, p. 73, show-ing this type of villa with a large loggia and the dispo-sition of rooms behind it.

Most of Palladio's villas are less theoretical in plan and design and, on the whole, more vigorous in their entire treatment. When the large colonnaded loggia is placed at the front of the house there is seldom a room of the same width behind it. Usually there is a narrower and deeper one along the main axis and on either side of that other rooms with windows which, in good Vicenza fashion, are placed near the corners.

This is true of Villa Piove-ne, p. 73.

From outside you are aware of a certain regularity but it is not as rigid as when the windows are disposed according to a regular rhythm, at definite intervals. It is like music in which the rhythm is not accentuated by distinct beats. The double windows which appear to be joined together are, actually, ordinary single windows separated, inside, by a wall. The colonnaded portico seems to hold the rooms behind it together, like a huge clamp, and at the same time it produces interesting variations of light and shade indoors and on the façade. The portico, too, has its small irregularities compared with the classical prototype. The centre pair of columns, above the entrance, are more widely spaced than the others. Again a comparison with music suggests itself, as when the execution of a composition gives an impression of something deeply felt and human in the performance.

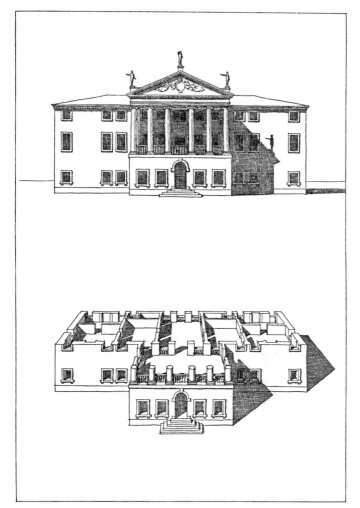

Andrea Palladio: Villa Pio-
vene, Lonedo. The façade
behind the portico is repro-
duced on a scale of 1 : 500.
The drawing has been con-
structed after an old en-
graving. In its present form
the villa has a large out-
side stairway which leads
down from the loggia on the
second-storey and around to
the magnificent garden-stair-
way, shown on p. 68.

Palladio's villas came to be regarded as examples of an ideal architecture. For him purely utilitarian considerations were of secondary importance, and the main problem was to create noble compositions of space and building masses, lavish in size but austere in materials and decoration. The large plane surfaces of wall, faced with stucco, are broken only by the dark window openings and in their extreme simplicity form an effective background for the shadow effects produced by the pillared porticoes and their finely executed details.

We obtain an impression of how people lived in such villas from the scenes of feasting painted by Palladio's contemporary, Paolo Veronese, who depicts aristocratic banquets amidst columns in a visionary architecture of loggias.

73

Palladio's villas, with their great architecture even in smaller works, marked a new epoch in European architectural history. Time and again architects have returned to them, now finding this feature of his art particularly important, now that. The composition of Villa Rotunda, with all rooms grouped symmetrically round a central hall, was an ever recurring ideal. In Vitruvius Britannicus quite a number of plates show country houses designed along the lines of Villa Rotunda. The vigorous quality of Palladian architecture, as shown in the fenestration and the general design and punctuation of façades, was sometimes admired, sometimes frowned upon. It appealed especially to Baroque architects with their lively sense of rhythm. But for everyone the villas were among the sights that must be seen, among the important monuments of Italy. And as a study trip to that country was not only almost obligatory for an artist but also a part of every gentleman's education, the influence of the villas in the neighbourhood of Vicenza soon spread all through western Europe.

An important variation of the Villa Rotunda *motif* appeared in France during the reign of Louis XIV. From his father, Louis XIII, the king had inherited a small, three-winged hunting chateau, Versailles, which he continued enlarging until it became a residence of enormous dimensions. It included not only an amazing collection of buildings but also a number of vast parks containing artificial lakes, fountains and many works of art. The Duke of Saint Simon, who lived at the end of the reign of the *Grand Monarque,* wrote in his memoirs (which are exceedingly malicious and hardly do the king justice) : "The king, who became tired of all this magnificence and the endless stream of people, persuaded himself that he now and then longed for something small and solitary. He searched the neighbourhood of Versailles for a spot that would satisfy this new craving for solitude ... Behind Louveciennes he found a deep, narrow valley, inaccessible because of swamps, with no view, and with a wretched village called Marly on one of the slopes. The complete seclusion of this tract, where there was no view or the possibility of creating one, was just what made it acceptable ... The hermitage was built. Its sole purpose was to provide a place where the king could spend three nights, from Wednesday to Saturday, two or three times a

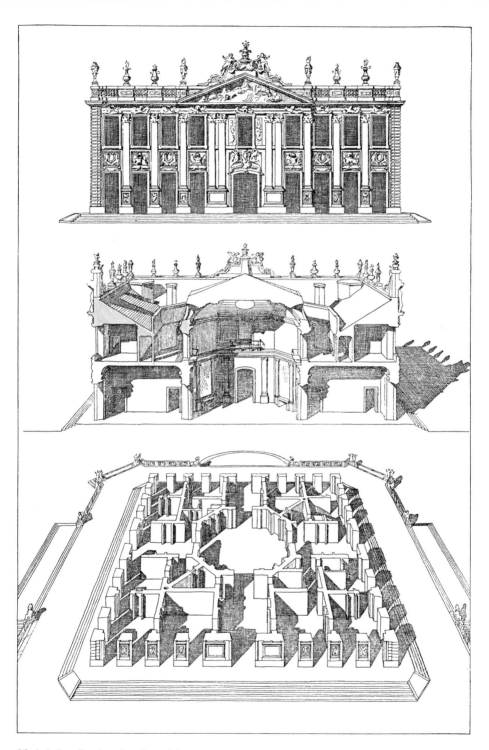

Marly le Roy. Façade and section scaled to 1 : 500.

75

year, together with a dozen of the most indispensable attendants. Little by little the hermitage was enlarged; between each new building operation slopes were cleared to make place for the new construction and finally the last one was cut away to obtain some semblance of a view, even though constricted and not very attractive." Saint Simon goes on to describe the great operations that were carried out, involving buildings, gardens, fountains, mirror ponds, and the enormous aqueduct, called "Marly's machine", which not only supplied Marly with water but also the fountains and cascades of Versailles. Toward the end of his life the king spent most of his time there. Marly was no ordinary little hermit's dwelling. The drawing on page 75 shows the main building which may not seem very impressive. But all its dimensions were colossal, as can easily be verified by comparing it with the other buildings drawn to the same scale. For instance, Marly's two storeys are as high as the six of the Copenhagen apartment blocks on page 158. The main edifice was a rectangular building of two storeys, much larger in ground plan than Villa Rotunda. The rooms were grouped around an octagonal domed hall rising through both storeys. But in France, where earlier there had been towers and domes on all palaces, the taste, now, was so opposed to any construction above the crowning cornice that the dome of Marly was drawn down into the building block. The room received light from a hidden passage built around the dome. The composition of Marly was admirably clear, its architecture austere but very different from Versailles. The rectangular main building lay at the far end of an oblong mirror pond, surrounded by terraces and slopes. On either side of it a number af small houses were erected on the upper terrace, each one likewise rectangular in ground plan and formed as a perfect cube, containing simple lodgings for one of the court attendants. These pavilions were connected with each other by bowered walks so that, though standing singly, they nevertheless formed an architectural unit. At the lower end of the mirror pond cascades poured down to a new pond below and the entire estate was surrounded by forests and groves. After the death of Louis XIV Marly fell into disrepair and was later demolished so that now there is not a stone left of the hermitage.

Palazzo Farnese in Rome.
Scale 1 : 500.

THE DUTCH CONTRIBUTION

In Italy, as we have seen, the Baroque architect worked
with classic details, with columns and pilasters in plastic building masses, with fusions and penetrations, with vigorous contrasts of solids and voids, with bold sculpture, billowing marble
draperies, and mannered profiling. But nevertheless, throughout all periods the Italians showed great love of simplicity and
classic dignity. The noble ruins of antiquity were always before
their eyes. Stripped of all ornament these ancient monuments
were probably even more sublime than when they had been new.
Like an atavism, Michelangelo's great Baroque of the 16th
century appeared again in Bernini's work a hundred years later.
Both of these illustrious men were architects and sculptors at
the same time, both favoured a very vigorous and expressive
style but they also admired the simple, massive building block,
the great rectangular *palazzo*. From Rome this ideal moved
north to Paris, London, and Copenhagen, but did not take
root in any of these places. Not until it reached Stockholm
did the vision of the great cubic *palazzo* become a reality.

Italian travellers knew it from the *Palazzo Farnese,* in
Rome, a building that had been carried out in several stages
and finally crowned with Michelangelo's enormous cornice,
which emphasizes its magnitude. About 1650 Bernini built the
great *Palazzo Montecitorio* which is also massive in form and
Baroque in detail. Dramatically, it rises into the air as if grow-

77

*Stockholm in the 16th century. Scale 1 : 20.000.
North upward.*

*Central part of Stockholm in
the 19th century.
Scale 1 : 20.000.
North upward.*

ing out of the rocky ground. Below, it is of rugged ashlar skilfully arranged to resemble mighty blocks of natural stone. From this base the fine details of the building unfold themselves, just as a Rodin figure seems to evolve from the crystals of a block of marble. When Bernini was called to Paris to design the new Louvre, his plan had been to carry out this architectural vision on an even greater scale.

Christopher Wren, who visited Paris in 1665, saw Bernini's drawings and was fascinated by the great man. But in the England of the newly restored Charles II there was even less chance of carrying out the great Italian *palazzo*. The Merry Monarch was satisfied so long as he could remain on his throne and did not have to "go on his travels again", and he had no desire to risk his popularity by indulging in building projects. Copenhagen, like so many royal residential towns of the 17th century, lacked a palace that was in keeping with the pomp and splendour of Absolutism. In 1694 the famous Swedish architect, Nicodemus Tessin the Younger, was invited to the Danish capital to submit plans for a new royal residence. He too, was a great admirer of Bernini whom he had met in Rome. The only result of his magnificent plans, however, was a gigantic wooden model, on a scale of half an inch to the foot, which was kept for over a century and admired by many architects. When finally the time did come for the erection of a new palace (Christiansborg 1733-40), its great form was reminiscent of Tessin's model — an offshoot of the cubic Italian *palazzo* — even though, in detail, it bore the stamp of southern German Baroque (Illustrated page 117).

*Stockholm seen from the east.
To the right: The old castle.
After an engraving from the
17th century.*

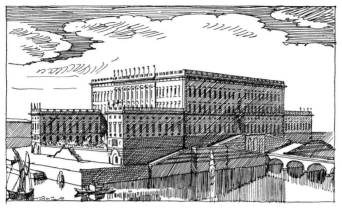

*Stockholm. The Royal Castle,
designed by Nicodemus Tessin the Younger (18th century).*

The true descendant of the Italian *palazzo* was to appear
for the first time in Stockholm. At this period the Swedish
capital was a small, medieval town on a rocky island that raised
its ridge high above the sea. At the top the market-place was
situated, separated from the church by a single building block.
It was a 13th-century planned town of the New Brandenburg
type (see p. 17), but less regular, due to the varying levels.
Originally the town had been very small, surrounded by protective walls which fortified the tremendous acclivity from the
low-lying coast to the town perched high above it. But soon
the houses of great merchants sprang up outside the walls, with
their gabled fronts cheek by jowl along the quayside. Today we
can still see the old town rising above a palisade of gabled
buildings. Between the old houses, plastered in yellow ochres
and reds, steep, narrow alleys lead to the top of the hilly island,
as in Italian towns. And now the gigantic cubic form of the
new palace was added to the town, standing four-square and
firmly planted, in contrast to the myriads of coloured prisms
which, together, form a strangely animated body.

Just as this far northern city awakens memories of an Italian
town, its palace is a complete apotheosis of the Italian *palazzo*.
Nowhere else can we see more clearly the terrace-like construction, rising from the rugged stone base to the finely executed Corinthian cornice at the top. During the many years the
Swedish soldier king, Charles XII, campaigned all over Europe, he was in constant correspondance with the architect
about the magnificent palace growing out of the bleak, rocky
island far away to the north.

*Stockholm. The Royal Castle;
the north façade seen from
the sunken garden "Ström-
parterren". Compare Villa
d'Este p. 67.*

79

In the same manner, all the monarchies and duchies of
Europe were doing all in their power to raise great palaces
which would dominate their small, ancient capitals. But at
one place, in the republican Netherlands, in the wealthy city of
Amsterdam, the burghers succeeded in creating, *not* an impressive palace, but an impressive city. While it entirely lacked
the one dominating body, every building in it was part of a
harmonious whole, the entire city one great composition. And
Amsterdam's houses were, contrary to all the tendencies of the
period, light below and heavy above, not made of stone but
of wood and brick, glistening with oil and colour and tar
like well kept ships.

In the Netherlands the houses repudiated the building principles of other countries, not because the architects wanted to be
different but because it was necessary. For centuries the Dutch
had lived at constant war with the elements, with storms and
the sea. Other countries had natural riches, easily exploited.
The mere fact of owning land meant wealth. But in Holland
nothing came easily. The very land, itself, had to be wrested
from nature by a technique which had quickly reached a high
stage of development: the building of dikes, the digging of
canals, the draining of land lying below the level of the sea.
Wealth had to be worked for, in shipping, fishing and trade.
All this resulted in a nation of enterprising and energetic people
who had learned to depend on their own resources.

A. J. Barnouw: The Mak-
ing of Modern Holland.
London, 1948.

In *The Making of Modern Holland,* A. J. Barnouw writes:
"The Dutchman is by nature a rugged individualist. But rugged individualism does not make for civil liberty." He explains
that "the Dutch, who for various reasons, physical, economic,
or political, joined their individual lives into communal units,
learned by bitter experience that their strength lay in co-operation, and that co-operation was feasible only if all agreed to
limit their personal liberties by common obedience to self-made
laws. By the end of the Middle Ages the majority of the Dutch
people were living in urban centres. In 1500 Holland and
Belgium numbered no fewer than 208 fortified towns and 150
large villages which, but for the lack of walls, might pass for
towns." Many of Holland's towns were built on the reclaimed
floor of the sea, the so-called polders. To secure building land
at all, it was first necessary to dig canals, using the earth thus

Oude&elft est fra Oude Kerk 10·9·1950.

obtained to erect dikes around areas that had been filled up with sand brought there from long distances. And the erection of a house was no less toilsome. Piles had to be driven into the earth below ground-water, to procure a firm foundation. Then a constant water-level had to be provided, to secure the piles from rotting and all the houses from collapsing. The first communal institution these individualists had to agree upon was a waterlevel office, whose duty it was to keep the water of canals and sluices at a permanent level.

In the historical town of Delft, the stateliest of all houses is still the quite Gothic "Gemeenlandshuis", where the water-level office is still found; a building from c. 1520 with tower and spire and colourful coats-of-arms on the façade.

This venerable building faces Delft's main waterway, the Oude Delft canal. Here we see the typical beginnings of a Dutch town: a stone walled canal with building blocks above it on each side, covered with houses built closely together and separated from the canal by cobbled roadways. The narrow, gabled ends of the houses face the canal and behind the deep houses are gardens. The side walls are the supporting ones. The houses lie so closely together that two can share the same piling, thereby reducing the heavy construction costs. All floor joists rest on the side walls so that the front and back walls bear no other weight than their own. By making these end walls light, not only is the cost of piling reduced but the walls can be filled with windows so that daylight can penetrate the deep rooms. The idea of piercing the façades with many open-ings, like fretwork, is an old one in Holland. Even today, you can see a Dutch house being built in which side walls, floors and roof are completed before the façade walls are set in place, as in a doll's house. The most important features of the façades are the heavy window sills, which are set up before the inter-vening spaces are filled in with brick. In contrast to the classic building method, where the walls are of paramount importance and windows simply openings in the compact mass, the Dutch method seems like putting the cart before the horse. But in Holland the windows, and not the expanse of brick, form the outer walls.

In Delft, at a right angle to the Oude Delft Canal — which runs approximately north-south — a fine market-place extends almost from the massive, old church, *Oude Kerk,* built about 1250, which leans out over the canal, to the newer *Nieuwe Kerk,* from about 1381. When Delft flourished about the year 1600 as one of the largest cities of the Netherlands, the build-ings along the market-place were a continuous row of large shops. An engraving of 1732 shows that in the entire row of medieval gabled houses there was not one with brick walls at the ground floor level. They were houses built on piles, and the piling was simply continued to the second or third storey, above which the brickwork began.

Something of the same sort was found in Venice, where the houses, at lower level, were a net of thin columns and lace-like stonework; higher up, the walls became more solid. In the Dutch climate there was no need for colonnades. The lower storeys were closed with windows, which let the light in and kept the cold out. In early days glass was so expensive that panes were installed only in the upper half of windows; the lower half was provided with wooden shutters. Later, glass was also set in below. The new panes were put in behind the shutters, which were kept so that the inhabitants could control light and temperature as well as exclude the stares of the inquisitive. In some houses indoor shutters were added to the upper half of the windows. Curtains, too, came into use. In this way, the rooms had not only as much window space as a modern, functional house, but at the same time there were greater possibilities of regulating and varying the lighting, all

Typical Dutch town houses from the 16th century with stepped gables. The ground floor façade is a wooden framework filled in with glass panes and shutters.

*The Market Place in Delft.
After an engraving from 1732
by Leon Schenk from a painting by A. Rademaker. In the
corner building to the right
lived the painter Vermeer.*

the way from the bright light of a studio to the most dramatic *clair-obscur,* with light from a single pane concentrated on one spot in the room. In other words, it was possible not only to regulate the *quantity* of light but also the *quality.* And never before or since have the artists of any country utilized to better advantage the possibilities architecture offered them.

The Dutch painters had their own world of motives, shared by no others. While Louis XIV's court painter, Le Brun (1619-1690), created for the court surroundings consisting of allegories of Alexander the Great and his men or Greek gods on Mount Olympus, the Dutch individualists decorated their walls with canvases depicting their own daily lives. Figure groups were studies from life, carefully posed in relation to the light so that the greatest possible brilliancy was reflected in the officer's uniform and the silk and velvet of the maiden's gown. The pictures were painted for an expert clientele of merchants who knew all about rich fabrics. The figures are grouped against a background of solid wealth, dimly lighted interiors with huge renaissance cupboards or canopied beds like small houses of curtains and draperies. Often the background is toned down so it will not vie with the livelier colours of the fore-ground — and where the painters, themselves, have left off, museum conservators of the Romantic period have finished by almost obliterating the background with an artificially dark-ened varnish.

But it is a mistake to believe that these dimly lighted interiors give any impression of Dutch homes with their white plastered walls and large windows. One painter, alone, has recorded for us the freshness and sound taste of those light rooms: Johannes Vermeer of Delft (1632-1675).

83

*Among the many valuable
books on Johannes Vermeer
the biography by the Dutch art
historian P. T. A. Swillens
published in English by Spec-
trum Utrecht Brussels 1950
is specially recommended for
its exact data and information on the conditions under
which Vermeer's pictures
were created.*

*Delft, Oude Langendijk with
the house in which Vermeer
died, seen from the tower of
Nieuwe Kerk.*

In the same town, a few doors away, Vermeer's contemporary, Anthony van Leeuwenhoek (1632-1723), constructed
microscopes and employed them with so much imagination and
thoroughness that he entirely changed the conception of the
human organism; he studied blood corpuscles and capillaries
and was the first to observe and draw bacteria. With the same
thoroughness, Vermeer concentrated on his studies of human
figures seen in relation to a room. The room was his studio,
one of those simple Dutch rooms with a tiled floor that clearly
registered all depths and the position of each individual object
between the planes of the picture and the rear wall. The last
window in the side wall to the left was placed right up in the
corner so that a strong, clear side light fell on the rear wall —
of white plaster and a row of Delft tiles — varying in intensity
from the greatest brilliance nearest the window to a dim patch,
above at the right. But by regulating the shutters of the window, or hanging yellow or blue curtains before it, Vermeer
could change the lighting and make the rear wall a coloured
or a dark background. In this way he was able to paint innumerable variations of daylight, which, in his room, where
the direct rays of the sun did not penetrate, was always cool
and clear. In the foreground he could hang draperies from the
beamed ceiling, thus framing that bit of the room he wished to
depict. In these mathematically exact surroundings, Vermeer
arranged his figures and a few accessories, such as tables, chairs,
musical instruments, oriental rugs, and other objects that show
up well in a clear light. In Rembrandt's or Frans Hals'
pictures, black may mean a very dark shadow. Such dark shadows are not found in Vermeer's paintings. Even that side
which is not lighted receives so much reflected light from the
white walls that its colour is clearly observed. In this way, even
walls which are not seen in the pictures play their part. We
are not only aware of the space *behind* the form but also *around*
it. There *is* black in his pictures but only on objects which
really are black; a black frame on the wall, a black beaver hat.
Thus, black becomes one more colour in addition to the yellows
and blues Vermeer shows such great partiality for, and, by
contrast, emphasizes their tones.

And how he experimented with the arrangement of his
figures in deliberate contrasts of light and shadow or in har-

*Reconstruction of the room
in which Vermeer painted
his famous interiors.*

monious groups built up from the chequered tile floor! How
carefully he placed chairs and violoncellos according to dia-
gonals on the floor of this simple room to emphasize its depth.
His choice of motives is limited; even meagre, compared to
those of contemporary French painters. But what rich tones
he has coaxed forth from his fine-toned instrument! It is quite
natural to think of his painting in terms of music. His values
consist entirely in proportions and relations between form and
space, between light and shadow, between colour tones. His
pictures are among the rarest things in art — only some thirty
of them have come to light, some quite small, but in each one
he has minutely studied and analyzed a new, picturesque
motive with infinite skill.

These *spirituel* canvases, without narrative, anecdote, or
as a romantic mind would put it, "without soul", revealed to
his fellow countrymen the beauty of their daily surroundings.
They were a purge for other painters. Pieter de Hooch (1629-
c. 1684), who had painted a number of *genre* pictures of no
particular merit, entirely changed after coming to live in Delft.
It is impossible not to feel that the ideal endeavours of Vermeer
influenced his work. He is, however, no mere imitator of his
colleague. While the latter painted in a cool, northern light,
Pieter de Hooch shows us rooms facing west, in which a sink-
ing sun casts a golden glow over the entire interior. He is
not satisfied with a single room but always plays upon the
effects to be obtained by looking from one room into another.

He must have painted his pictures in houses on the west side
of the Oude Delft canal. There are still, today, many large

85

*Old gardens in Delft seen
from a house at Oude Delft
(Huis Lambert van Meerten).*

and small gardens to be found there. Though probably not one
of de Hooch's canvases gives a correct picture of a particular
spot in Delft, every one of them gives a true impression of the
particular atmosphere of the town. He reveals to us the charm
of those burgher houses with their high-ceilinged, sober chambers, facing the long, tree-lined canal streets, and opening at
the rear on small, square gardens which, with their tables and
benches, are like cosy, outdoor rooms. Out there, well-protected from the elements and the inquisitive glances of strang-
ers, the family could sit and enjoy peaceful summer evenings
under leafy trees, while the nearby church towers in the
afterglow of the setting sun rang out their dulcet chimes.

De Hooch's work enjoyed great popularity. Time and time
again he painted the same motives with only small variations.
About 1667 he left Delft for Amsterdam but he never succeeded in depicting "the spirit of Amsterdam" so truly as he has
shown us Delft. Amsterdam could not be given in one picture.
Already in the 17th century it had become too large and too
wealthy for that.

In the south-eastern part of the old town there is a group
of dwellings known as *Begijnhof* which, within a small area,
contains a retrospective collection of Amsterdam houses as they
developed from the Gothic period to the Baroque. Actually, it
is a sort of foundation for the poor of the parish, where each
family has its own house. The houses have been built in a ring
around a church so that they form a peaceful close, shutting

Houses at Begijnhof in Amsterdam. The two houses to
the left with the typical
"halsgevel" breaking through
the horizontal cornice of the
Baroque façade.

out the traffic of the streets. In true Dutch fashion it is a communal and an individual housing scheme at one and the same
time. Standing at the entrance, which is a narrow stone passage
through one of the houses, is a high-gabled, Gothic dwelling
built entirely of wood. But even this old house has an amazing
amount of window space. Most of the other houses have been
rebuilt several times. The ground storeys of some of them are
enclosed entirely by windows and some have the special Amsterdam gable, the *halsgevel,* with a large loft to which
furniture and wares are hoisted.

Amsterdam, Begijnhof No. 4,
a high gabled Gothic dwelling built entirely of wood.

While the development of Delft stagnated and the town
lived on its past, Amsterdam grew into a city of unusual size.
The town was built on the mouth of a river. On each side of
the Amstel a dike was erected, forming the foundation of a
very modest settlement. Along the ridges ran the narrow main
streets; stretching down to the river wharves were rows of
merchants' houses, and around it all were palisades and moats,
still surviving in canal and street names in Amsterdam, such
as *Oude Zijds Achterburgwaal.*

From this nucleus, Amsterdam was to expand in an unusually organic fashion. Around the original dikes and canals new
dikes and new canals were laid out in advance so that there
would always be effective water connections with all houses.
If this had been carried out piecemeal, the result would have
been a city without form or unity. Instead, plans were laid,
about the year 1612, for systematic expansion during the
following centuries — *not* according to international town
planning ideals but following a system which was to become
characteristic of Amsterdam.

87

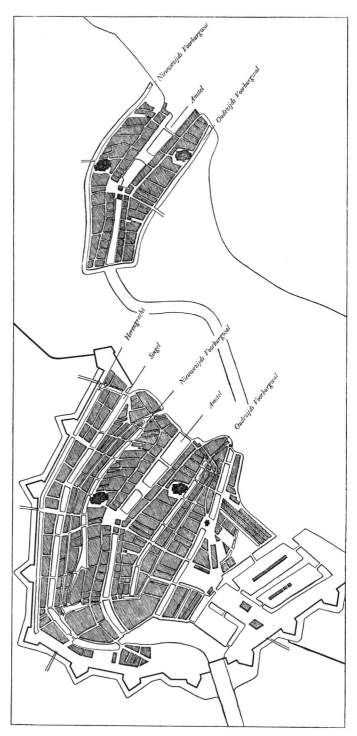

The City of Amsterdam in three stages. Scale 1 : 20.000. North upward. On this page : Above, Amsterdam about 1400 on both sides of the river Amstel. The oldest part to the east with Oude Kerk, the younger part to the west with Nieuwe Kerk. Below, Amsterdam about 1600. Page 89, Amsterdam in the 19th century enlarged according to the great plan of 1612.

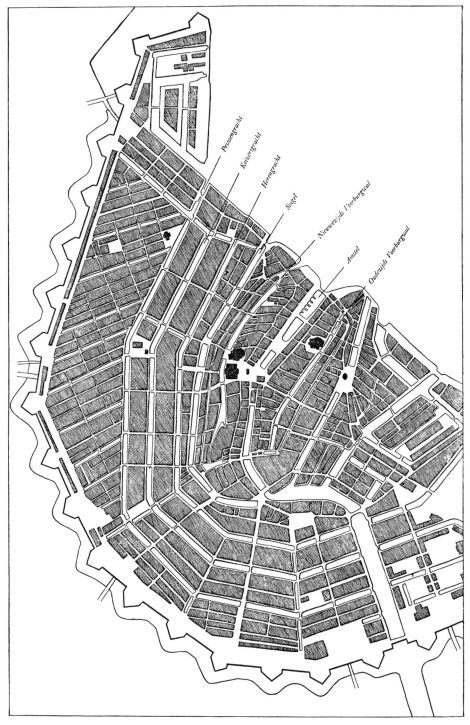

Prinsengracht

Keizersgracht

Herengracht

Singel

Nieuwezijds Voorburgwal

Amstel

Oudezijds Voorburgwal

Heerengracht in Amsterdam.

Just as the great cubic palace in a royal residential city became a symbol of Absolutism, Amsterdam became the true symbol of the Dutch Commonwealth. In older Dutch towns an imposing town hall, pinnacled and spired, over-shadowed all the small houses. But in this new city great architectonic unity was created by the rows of wealthy burgher houses along the canals. The tree-lined canals and the unified block fronts of solid, unpretentious houses reflected the diligence and energy of this Dutch community and the commercial genius of its people. The town was like a great and flourishing corporation in which each citizen owned shares.

The unit was not a cloistered court, as in the medieval *Begijnhof,* but a long, broad canal through which heavily laden barges brought merchandise to and from the houses. The Dutch had become masters of the art of canal-building. Large stretches of water, branches of the Zuider Zee, were changed into meadow land in the 16th and 17th centuries. On a detailed map of Holland they are easily recognizable by their regular net of straight-flowing canals. The many windmills, which became an organic part of the Dutch landscape, harnessed the wind to pump water from canals at one level up into other canals at another level and finally out into the sea. Just as the Dutch painters found beauty in their meadow lands and flower beds converted from the floor of the sea, Dutch town planners saw the architectonic possibilities of the canal streets.

Long before Claude Lorrain, in the 17th century, painted

Keizersgracht in Amsterdam.

his heroic landscapes with deep perspectives built up from the water surface of a harbour or sea, and long before Le Nôtre laid out his parks at Vaux-le-Vicomte and Versailles around great canals in a flat landscape, Amsterdam had been planned as a city of canal vistas, built in rings, one beyond the other. First to be carried out were the three broad, concentric canals: innermost, the Heerengracht, then the Keizersgracht and finally the Prinzengracht. (Though the existence of kaisers and princes was recognized, the burghers of the city came first.)

Compared to the canals of Delft, these were given enormous dimensions. The basins of the Heerengracht and of the Prinzengracht are almost 80 feet broad while that of the Keizersgracht is actually 88 feet. The distance between the rows of houses on either side of the canal is over 150 feet (in comparison, the distance between facing buildings in Whitehall, at the broadest part, is about 140 feet, and in Portland Place in London 124 feet). And between the houses and the canal, on each side, is a broad quay street, paved with various kinds of cobbling according to the use to which the several stretches are put. Nearest the canal it is often of rough granite cobblestone, laid in areas about 10 feet broad. Here, merchandise from the barges is stacked, and in this area trees are planted. The middle stretch is the roadway, paved with clinker bricks which are often laid in a herring-bone pattern down the centre with narrower strips in another pattern on each side for pedestrians. Finally, just

See "Amsterdamse Stoepen"
door Ir A. Boeken. Amsterdam
1950.

outside the houses, is a special area called, in Amsterdam, the "stoep", which is partly a pavement and partly a sort of threshold of the house. The house, itself, cannot be built upon the stoep but it may be used for the cellar entrance or for the stairway up to the high ground floor. The entrance staircases in Amsterdam are often works of art, carried out in magnificent *bleu belge* stone-work which forms a striking contrast to the dark red brick of the houses. These staircases are often furnished with finely executed cast-iron hand-rails. When not taken up by the stairway or other projections, the stoep is raised a step above the roadway and paved with fine tiles or other decorative facing. As it is actually part of the house, the owner takes pride in keeping his stoep as immaculate as possible. Every morning, in front of all the houses, there is a scrubbing and flushing of stairways and stoeps like that on board the most shipshape of vessels. On the whole, the visitor is always being reminded that he is in a city in which shipping plays an important rôle. The walls of the houses are built of small, dark red bricks. These walls are often no more than eight inches thick and, to keep out the damp, are treated with linseed oil, which deepens the colour of the brick and makes the walls shine like the sides of a ship. The woodwork stands out clearly from the dark walls. The broad sills and narrow window frames are carefully harmonized in two colours: cream and white, white and dark green, or grey and white. When you add to all this the gilded and polychrome signs which are reminiscent of gallion figures in their colours and shape, and the fact that the entire building is frequently spruced up with paint and oil, you get a colourful street scene aptly suited to this maritime city. The houses are tall and narrow. They lean a bit forward. Is this a tradition from the Gothic period with its corbelled storeys or does it spring from the painted side of a ship? The floor of the ground storey is raised many steps above the street and the ground storey, itself, is of impressive dimensions. Higher up, the storeys diminish in size and at the top there is a loft or two for the storing of merchandise. These attract attention by a large hoisting beam projecting from the gable. This is, indeed, found on all houses, even those which have no loft, for the interior staircases are so narrow and steep that it is impossible to carry furniture up through the house.

*Amsterdams Bouwkunst en
Stadsschoon 1306 — 1942 door
J. G. Wattjes & F. A. War-
ners, Amsterdam 1944, with
858 illustrations gives a detailed description of houses
old and new.*

By following the *grachter* it is possible to study the changing styles of the expanding city. But actually the resemblance of the houses to each other is stronger than their differences, which are revealed more by architectural details than by structural dissimilarity. Gabled Renaissance houses with their corbel-steps seem half-gothic, and even when the façades of the 17th century were decorated with classic pilasters, and cornices, the spacious windows were retained and huge gables shot into the air above the crowning cornices, with loft openings and projecting hoisting beams. And added to all this were great baroque ornaments, such as scrolls and festoons, or, more typical of Amsterdam, a pair of white dolphins standing on their heads on either side of the red brick loft dormer, and supporting it with their magnificently curved tails.

Here, as in Delft, the houses have deep rooms. But everything in Amsterdam is on a larger scale. The rooms are seldom symmetrically arranged as this is difficult to accomplish in a narrow gabled house. Instead, they open on each other in a quite casual manner that is very effective, giving the house a pleasing variety of light and dark, large and small rooms. There is usually a large room facing the street, with immense windows, and behind it there may be a small, dimly lighted cabinet with only one window looking out on a deep, diminutive court. Behind this, again, a light and airy room leads to a snug garden, idyllically concealed behind the house. It is like one of Pieter de Hooch's pictures in which there is always a little glimpse of a room behind the one he has painted, an enticing glimpse that awakens the joy of expectation. Such expectations are awakened at many places in Amsterdam. You look down a long, straight canal street ending in a cambered bridge which, at the same time, frames the opening to a new stretch of canal turning in another direction and leading further into this delightful city which is ever the same and ever new.

In the excellent Dutch series: Heemschutserie, are popular illustrated books on Amsterdam by A. A. Kok, "Amsterdamsche Woonhuizen" "De historische Schoonheid van Amsterdam".

CHARLOTTENBORG

The city culture of Holland spread to England, Denmark and Sweden in the wake of Dutch trade. When the young men of these countries made *the grand tour* Holland was included in their itineraries. And they were amazed when they discovered that Dutch merchants had more comfort and more of the paraphernalia of wealth in their narrow, gabled houses in Amsterdam, than many a great nobleman had, at home, in his palace. At the end of the 17th century and during the first decades of the 18th English architecture was strongly influenced by Holland. Not only are the materials and architectural details pure Dutch but there is something in the disposition of the houses in relation to the street that is reminiscent of Holland. In London an "area" appeared before every house with steps leading up to the first floor, corresponding to the *stoep* in Holland. But in England there was also a small, sunk court that gave access to the basement where the kitchen was located. In Holland, of course, no basement was possible because of the high water-table.

In Stockholm Dutch building traditions were brought to the country by wealthy noblemen. The first plans for the headquarters of nobility in Stockholm, *Riddarhuset,* (House of Lords) had been made by French architects. But when the time came to build, a well-known Dutch architect, Justus Vingboons of Amsterdam, was engaged for the work and

94

Riddarhuset became a red brick building with tall pilasters. On its completion Vingboons returned to Amsterdam where he built a double house for the two brothers Trip, *Trippenhuis,* of similar design but even more splendid than the Stockholm building.

His brother, Phillipe Vingboons, was responsible for many houses in Amsterdam and his work became known far and wide through engravings of the buildings. They are, for the most, commodious town houses in a budding Baroque adapted to Dutch conditions. The largest of his projects, plans for a new Amsterdam town hall, was, however, never carried out. (Instead, Jacob van Campen's heavy stone edifice was chosen, a building which, with its great pilasters and columns, resembles two buildings, one above the other).

This unrealized project had its importance, nevertheless. It became the model for the first great royal residence to be built in Copenhagen after the Danish king became an absolute monarch in 1660. Until then, Copenhagen had been a small town with a medieval network of narrow, crooked streets. But plans were ready for its expansion to double its size. The fortifications were already enlarged and a grid-iron system of streets had been adapted for the new part of the town. The crown owned most of the land in question and it was the king's urgent desire that the new district be worthy of a royal residential city. Immediately beyond the old eastern gateway to the town a large *place* was laid out, *Kongens Nytorv* (the Kings's New Plaza) which was to unite the old town with

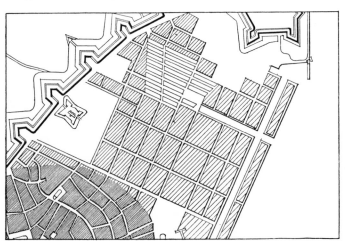

New-Copenhagen after a project from c. 1660. Scale c. 1:20.000. North upward. The darker hatching shows the old town. At left Rosenborg Castle standing close to the city wall, further toward the northeast "Nyboder", small houses built by Christian IV for seamen's families.

95

the new. In the centre of it an equestrian statue of the king, in the guise of a Roman imperator, was raised and, as a background for the statue, a large town residence was to be erected for the king's illegitimate son, Ulrik Frederik Gyldenløve (which means Golden Lion), who was viceroy of Norway.

This building is worth studying. It shows how the period combined several prototypes in one structure. In it we find traces of the Senators' Palace in Rome, of the Palais de Luxembourg in Paris and of Phillipe Vingboon's Amsterdam town hall project. At the same time it forms a connecting link between the age when a royal residence was a fortified castle and the period of Absolutism, when the great of the world felt themselves secure enough to live in modern, comfortable dwellings with large, light rooms.

Gyldenløve (1638—1704) was a true representative of his time. He had received the best education the period afforded. At the age of ten he had been sent to Paris where he was tutored until he entered the University of Siena in 1654. When he was 19 years old he was made a colonel of the Danish army. He was a gay, dashing soldier, full of ambition and energy, intelligent, well-informed, of cultivated taste, a skilled fencer, and a great beau.

Together with his half-brother, the Danish crown prince, who was seven years his junior, he made the grand tour in 1661, visiting Holland, Belgium, France, and Madrid. A connoisseur of food and wines — of which he could stand more than most — he amused himself mightily at the French court. Louis XIV had not yet started his palace-building and Ulrik Gyldenløve's own palace, which had not yet been planned, was to be influenced during its construction by the successive architectural developments of the age.

Charlottenborg — the foundations of which were laid in 1672 — was not conceived as a stronghold but was, nevertheless, originally designed with four turrets from which the façades and even the portal could be raked by gun-fire. The palace is shown as a building with domed towers on a medal struck to commemorate the laying of the corner-stone, and in an old drawing of the building. Such, then, was the original plan. But before it was completed, Charlottenborg had been transformed into a block with projecting end bays like the

The medal struck to commemorate the laying of the corner-stone of Charlottenborg, ca. 1672.

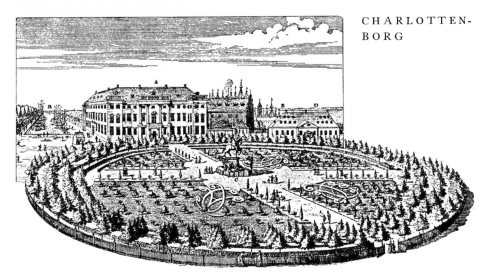

*Charlottenborg and "Kongens
Nytorv" with the equestrian
statue of king Christian V
Detail of an engraving by
Christoph Marselis.*

Palace of the Senators on Capitoline Hill in Rome, which, as
we have already seen (p. 42), had also originally been a
stronghold with corner turrets. There is one other faint resemblance between Charlottenborg and the Roman palace: both
were conceived as backgrounds for an equestrian statue standing on an open *place,* the equestrian guised as a Roman
imperator. But otherwise the Capitol and *Kongens Nytorv* are
just as different from each other as Rome and Copenhagen.
The piazza in Rome is constricted and takes full advantage
of the effects to be obtained from the steadily mounting
horizontal planes terminating in the tower above the Senators'
Palace. In Copenhagen, the *place* was created as a wide, open
garden, and both palace and statue are much more massive in
effect. Here, as in Holland, the flatness of the landscape has
been accentuated by a long canal, *Nyhavn,* which, running
parallel to the palace, brings the ships of the harbour right
into the town. From the statue, the long, horizontal axis
passes through the entrance, the courtyard, a new gateway,
and out to the deep Dutch garden. We can imagine the impression this great, open palace, with the unending, horizontal
vista, made on contemporary Danes coming from the narrow
streets of the older part of town where the houses stood in
long, compact rows.

Inside, the palace was more comfortable than a Roman
palazzo. Nevertheless, the owner, "His Exalted Excellency"
Ulrik Frederik Gyldenløve, in all his glory lacked many of the

97

*French bedchamber from be-
fore 1700, after a drawing
by Daniel Marot.*

conveniences quite ordinary people have today. Charlottenborg's large windows were a revolutionary departure. Its
rooms were large and light but in winter the palace, heated
only by open fires, was glacial. The only place where it was
sure to be warm was in bed and in Charlottenborg, as in all
dwellings north of the Alps, the bed chambers were quite
naturally of first importance. The more fashionable large
palace windows became, the more aristocracy suffered during
cold weather. In 1695 the Duke of Orleans wrote that it was
so cold in Versailles that wine and water froze in the glasses
on the king's table. Madame de Sevigné complains in one of
her letters that the ink is frozen in the inkwells. And when it
was so bad in France, how much worse it must have been in
the North! On winter days the magnificent salons of Charlottenborg were like icy caves. Only behind the drawn curtains
of the bed was protection from the withering cold to be found.
Thus the bed became a house within a house; the prince's bed
a tabernacle, a holy of holies. The more the absolute ruler was
worshipped as a divinity, the more sacred his bed became. It
was a ceremony and a great honour to approach the bedside
of the new deity which, like the altar in a church, stood behind
a rail. The Danish king, Frederik III, had a gilt balustrade
round his bed, other members of the royal family had silver-
plated ones.

The rooms of the main wing of Gyldenløve's palace are
symmetrically arranged around the great banqueting hall in
the centre (F); on either side the state bedrooms of His

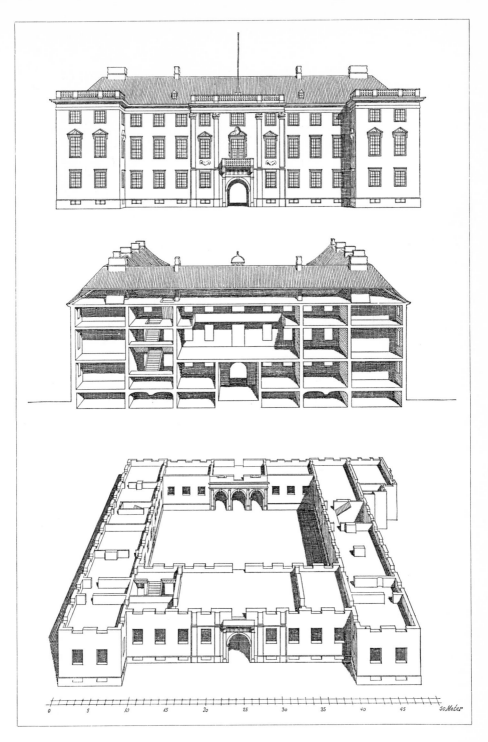

Charlottenborg. Façade scaled to c. 1:500.

99

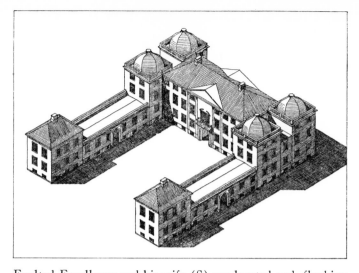

*Charlottenborg, plan scheme.
Scale c. 1 : 2.000.*

*Houghton Hall, Norfolk,
built for Sir Robert Wal-
pole by William Kent after
1722 is in details in the Palladian style, but in its out-
lines with the four domed
turrets it is of the same type
as the French and Swedish
buildings.*

Exalted Excellency and his wife (S) are located and, flanking
these, are two large, regular chambers, each 24 feet square.
In the room designed to be Gyldenløve's bed-chamber there is
still a very magnificent stucco ceiling with painted panels and
a large eagle spreading its wings above the bed site. The old
drawings and the corner-stone medallion, showing the palace
with domed corner turrets instead of the flat-roofed end bays,
give no idea of the original plan for the structure as a whole.
It would not be easy to place domes on the present building.
The original design must have been different. We can get
some idea of it by comparing Charlottenborg with somewhat
older Swedish or French palaces built with a tower or large
pavilion at each of the four corners of the main wing. Stockholm's old town hall, the Bonde palace, is shown in Dahlberg's
Svecia with four domed turrets. Today it stands with projecting end bays, just like Charlottenborg, but down near the
water there are two domed pavilions resembling those shown
on the old drawings of the Danish palace. Marie de Medici's
Palais de Luxembourg (see p. 62) is of the same type. It
belongs to the period when great palaces were composed of a
number of individual units instead of being united under one
roof. Gyldenløve was familiar with the Luxembourg as well
as with a number of other French palaces of the same style.
His Copenhagen residence was originally planned with four
domed turrets that were to contain the square rooms now
flanking the two state bedrooms, and the thickness of the palace

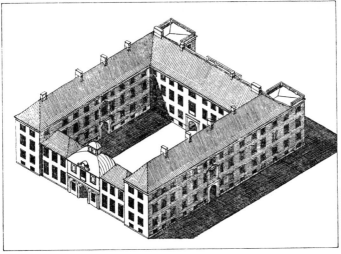

Chartottenborg's buildings as they stand today with three equally high wings and a fourth composed of three two-storey pavilions.

walls indicates that the side wings were to have been lower than the present ones, each one probably ending in a higher, pavilion-like structure. But as so often happened when palaces were under construction, it became evident that it had been planned too small for the household it was to contain. Gyldenløve had secretaries, a postmaster, accountants, a major-domo, cooks, lackeys, maids, etc. To make room for this huge staff, all three wings were carried up to the same height and covered with one roof. Oddly enough, only the fourth wing with the domed hall, which was the last to be built, has retained the character of a separate building with its own hipped roof.

Charlottenborg has many antecedents. The general impression is Italian, the disposition of its rooms is French, the material effect is Dutch. The walls are built of small, dark bricks in striking contrast to the light-coloured cornices and window frames. The window panes are flush with the walls. This is all quite Dutch. As a matter of fact Gyldenløve employed Dutch workmen on his palace just as his grandfather, Christian IV, had done when he built his.

But in Charlottenborg Copenhagen saw Baroque architectural ideals realized for the first time in the grouping of small and large rooms. The great banqueting hall, just over the central entrance, is two storeys high and this has been marked on the façade by tall pilasters. These giant orders together with the varying sizes of the windows not only give interest to the façade but clearly indicate the rhythmic variation of the

101

See drawing p. 99.

rooms behind: lower on the ground floor, very high in the middle, lowest at the top. The rooms vary in similar order on plan: the loftiest and most spacious in the centre with smaller ones on either hand — a rhythm of proportions of rich harmony, the whole bound together in unbreakable unity by long vistas through windows and doors.

Charlottenborg became the prototype for buildings in the new section of Copenhagen beyond the medieval line of fortifications. It was not so much the Dutch style or the details of the building that were copied. Indeed, a building with projecting end bays could not be used for town houses in street rows. But the composition of the building, with its high-ceilinged middle storey, like the Italian *piano nobile,* a lower ground storey and a still lower top storey with servants quarters, became typical of upper-class dwellings in the Danish capital throughout the 18th century. The type became so deeply rooted that the style of architecture was able to change from Baroque to Rococo and from Rococo to Classicism without changing this disposition of the plan. The design with a great hall and balcony in the centre was also kept as a type. The four magnificent Amalienborg palaces (see p. 131) were but a further development of the Charlottenborg composition. Here, the end bays have become very slight projections but the principal sub-divisions remain.

A TALE OF TWO CITIES

Paris and London represent two types of cities. Paris is the concentrated city in which many families live in each house. London is the scattered city in which one-family houses predominate, and where distances are great. One would naturally assume that the more a town grows, the greater becomes the necessity of crowding people together. But London, which is the second largest city in the world, proves otherwise. By and large, cities in England (but not in Scotland which, on this point, is very continental) and in America are the scattered type. Most of the cities on the Continent — though not all of them — are concentrated cities. The reasons for this are many. Here we have room only for a few indications which will help to characterize the two city types, Paris and London.

To a certain degree the special development of English towns can be attributed to the fact that England's best defence has always been her island location. Since 1066 the country has never been invaded. Therefore, it has not been necessary to surround English towns with constricting rings of fortifications, as was so often the case on the continent.

A city like Paris has expanded by placing one ring beyond the other, moving the line of defence further and further out. In the Middle Ages, in 1180, there was a wall around the island in the Seine — the Isle de la Cité — and small parts of the left and right banks. In 1370, the area of the city was enlarged by building a new wall on the right bank. The next expansion was due, not to the overcrowding of the city, but to the laying out of great royal gardens which broke through the city limits and formed a new boundary. This was carried further toward the northwest to protect the Tuileries gardens. Later, new rings were built around Paris, one in the 18th and one in the 19th centuries. The closed form continued to be regarded as absolutely necessary for a city. Building bans did not lead to a halt in the city's growth but only to the crowding of more people into each house.

London developed along quite different lines. Very early in its history the town within the Roman walls had become too small. At that time London was smaller than medieval

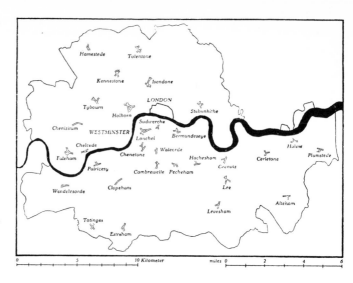

Villages near London mentioned in the Domesday Book from about the year 1080. Each village name signified a group of houses near a crossroad.

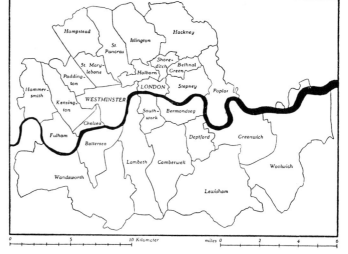

The boroughs which together form the County of London today. The nucleus of each borough is one of the old villages, every one of the names can be traced back to the Domesday Book.

Cologne or Paris. But new fortifications were not necessary. Instead, each village on the outskirts of old London became the nucleus of a new town. Together, they formed a cluster of towns which gradually have grown into one — and now there are plans to separate them again. The names of these villages, some of them found in the Domesday Book, were the same as those designating the boroughs which now form the community we call London. London is not a city in the sense that Paris is. It is a collection of towns. At many places within London two such towns are separated only by a street. Yet, when you go from one to the other there is a marked differ-

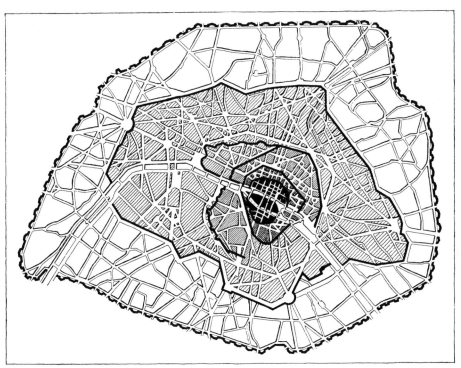

The development of Paris. Scale c. 1 : 100.000. North upward. Central core early Middle Ages, around this heavy black lines show boundaries of c. 1180, 1370, 1676, 1784—91 and 1841—45.

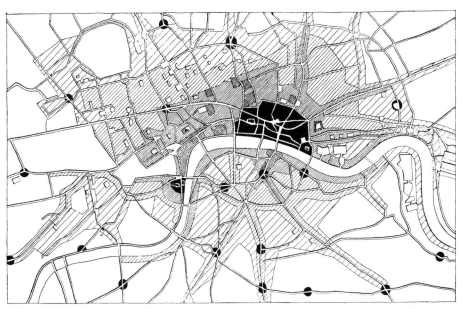

London's development. Scale c. 1 : 100.000. North upward. Black denotes inhabited districts in early Middle Ages. Cross-hatching later medieval settlements (convents, Temple, buildings in Westminster and London), finely hatched around these London c. 1660, thereafter c. 1790 and finally 1830.

View from a house in Rue de Turenne, Paris, toward houses on Place des Vosges, which seem so gothic with their soaring lines, high dormers and steep roofs.

ence. The inhabitants speak another dialect, they have different political views, different municipal authorities and rates, different ideas about the propriety of children using the swings and see-saws in the parks on Sunday. Every one of these towns has maintained local government to an extent which, in many instances, borders on the ridiculous. The two dominating towns were London proper, "the City of London", the seat of trade, and "the City of Westminster", the seat of government. The relations between these two have been decisive for England's history. The king (as well as the Government) does *not* reside in the City of London. When he comes there he is received with all the honours shown a foreign potentate visiting a free city. London's Lord Mayor comes to the spot where in older days the gate of the city stood and, with great ceremony, hands over to the king the keys of the gate which no longer stands there.

When Henri IV of France, as a building speculator on the grand scale, built the *Place Royale,* now the *Place des Vosges,* it was a new and epoch-making idea. This was early in the 17th century. (Henri IV died in 1610). At about the same time there lay a large, unbuilt area between London and Westminster where, earlier, a convent had stood. After the Reformation, Henry VIII had given the confiscated property to a nobleman who had been of great service to the royal house. Around 1630, this convent garden, or, as it is now called, Covent Garden, was ripe for exploitation and the fourth Earl of Bedford decided to utilize his land for a great building enterprise. But he wished to do it in just as stately a manner as the French king had carried out his building speculation. It was to be a monumental square with a church on its axis. The earl employed the country's first architect, Inigo Jones, to design the church and the façades of the buildings and to plan the arcades that were to surround the square. What was to be hidden behind the façades was left to the tenants to decide. The project turned out to be a much more classical, more Italian *place* than the Place des Vosges. The church was lower than all the other buildings but it seemed large because it had the largest detail, a great portico of columns. But this monumentality did not last very long. While the Place des Vosges became the scene of knightly sports and tournaments,

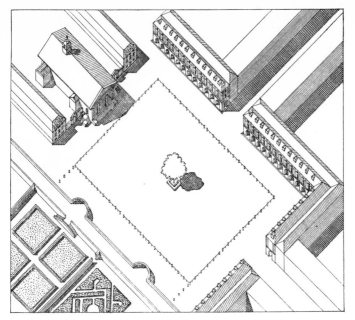

Covent Garden Square in London in its original form. In foreground, left, the Earl of Bedford's garden. Facing square St. Paul's Covent Garden, designed as a temple. The square was to be a classic forum with arcades and public meeting-place in the portico of the church.

Covent Garden became a vegetable market which filled the coffers of the Bedford family. In Paris the court took over the square, in London, trade — which gives a very good idea of part of the difference between the two cities.

The arcades of Covent Garden, however, really took on something of the same significance of the arcades of ancient market-places. They became a popular meeting place where friends strolled together, gossiping and discussing the news of the day. The arcade that led to some of the famous coffee houses and to the Covent Garden Theatre became a London institution and has left many traces in English art and literature.

These two real estate projects, Place des Vosges in Paris and Covent Garden in London, had many traits in common. But as time went on, the development of the two cities greatly diverged. Paris became more and more a consumer city, a place where the enormous fortunes, made on the great manorial estates of the aristocracy, were spent on luxuries. While there was a general decree prohibiting construction on hitherto unbuilt land, the government encouraged all building which served to glorify the monarchy. Therefore, if one wanted to build on an empty site, all that was necessary was to

107

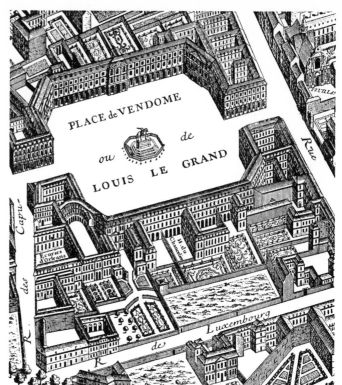

Place Vendôme, Paris. Section of Turgot's plan, 1731. In centre equestrian statue of Louis XIV with the magnificent, regular façade buildings around it — see p. 114 — which is in no way related to the buildings and courts behind.

fix upon a project which included a monumental *place* with a statue — and, lo! there was no longer any ban on building. It was even possible to obtain a subsidy from the government for the enterprise. This became the salvation of many a ruined nobleman, as for instance, the Duke de Vendôme. In 1677 his creditors got together to find out if they could not make something out of his large holdings. The architect Mansard drew up plans for a great building enterprise around a monumental place with a statue. It turned out to be a long, troublesome undertaking. The plans were changed several times. In 1699 Girardon's equestrian statue of Louis XIV was erected. The property then passed into the hands of the municipality which carried out the project according to the final plan. In 1701 the façades were finished and not until then did the sale of the building lots behind them begin. There was no connection between the façades and the houses they hid. On the other hand, the height of the houses was carefully adapted to the 17 meter high monument so that the equestrian statue was seen rising above the cornices.

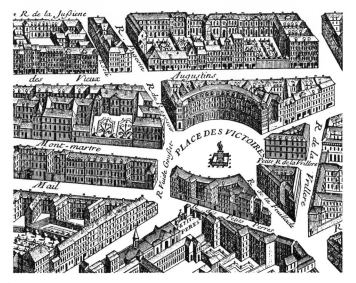

The Duke de la Feuillade also obtained permission to carry out a large building project around a circular plaza with a statue of Louis XIV. It was called the *Place des Victoires* and was laid out in 1697 just across the old city boundary, which had been pushed further out after the Cardinal's palace and the Tuileries had been built in the 16th century. (See p. 63). Instead of the usual equestrian statue, this time the monument was a standing figure of the king being crowned with laurels by the goddess of victory. It exists no longer. Like other royal monuments it was destroyed during the French Revolution.

The 18th century map of Paris shows other characteristic traits. Though the city's fortifications were no longer of vital importance, definite boundaries continued to be maintained. They were marked by the *Grands Boulevards*. The word "boulevard" is a corruption of the nordic *bulvirke* (bulwark) which means a palisade, a medieval form of defence work used before the employment of real walls and ramparts. The boulevard is the line of fortifications, itself, but when these were converted, in Paris, into broad, tree-lined wall streets, the designation "boulevard" was kept. And when, much later, under Napoleon III — as described in the chapter on Paris Boulevards — broad, radial thoroughfares, also planted with trees, were cut through the old city on all sides, these, too, were called boulevards. Today, the word simply means a broad, tree-lined avenue. However, in the 17th century the

109

boulevards were actually boundary lines beyond which buildings could not be erected because uncontrolled expansion of the city was considered very dangerous. The result was, naturally, that the population within the walls became more and more dense.

There were building bans in London, also, but no clearly defined city boundaries because the town had spread beyond the Roman walls so early in its history. It expanded particularly toward the west, until London and Westminster had completely merged. In the new districts there were many open spaces. These were of two kinds, originating from different causes. Some of them were old village greens and fields which, from time immemorial, had been set aside for the use for the inhabitants for sports, games and archery. Every form of custom and tradition has always been of great importance in England, where laws have never been collected into a logical system but have remained a simple record of rules and regulations naturally evolved from the daily life of the people. There are many accounts of the armed resistance of the inhabitants when building speculators attempted to exploit these old playing fields. They often became regular pitched battles with a number of wounded and even some dead. And in every case it was the defenders of the open spaces who held the field and won the support of the government. To this day there are still greens and commons spread all over London, where young people meet every Saturday all summer long, to play cricket, just as young people did when these green areas were parts of individual villages. In the centre of the city the open spaces that have been preserved have become playgrounds, bandstands, public tennis courts, and other areas of recreation.

The other type of open spaces came into existence in the course of great building speculations. Covent Garden, the first real "square" in London, was such a great success that others followed it. West of London's "City" lay a number of old manorial estates and country houses. As the urban development approached nearer and nearer, the grounds of these estates were parcelled out for building. The owners, however, desired to keep their old homes as long as possible, with sufficient open space around them, preferably toward the north where there was a splendid view of lovely, purpling hills crowned by the

⤛ *Portland Place laid out*
c. 1774 in a width of 100
feet so as not to take the
view toward the north
from Foley House.

⤛ *Bedford Square, c. 1775.*

⤛ *Soho Square, 1681.*

⤛ *Hanover Square, 1717.*

⤛ *Grosvenor Square, 1695.*

⤛ *Leicester Square, laid out*
for Leicester House in 1635.
⤛ *Berkley Square, 1698.*

⤛ *St. James Square, 1684.*

Section of London map, 1804.
Reproduced on a scale of
1 : 20.000. North upward,
The map shows a number of
the squares laid out in the
17th and 18th centuries.

old villages of Hampstead and Highgate. Therefore, a large
square was laid out in front of the house, which thus closed
the south side of the square; new buildings were erected on
the east and west sides, and the north side was kept open.
Later, as the district grew, the north side was also built up,
and a new London square had come into being.

III

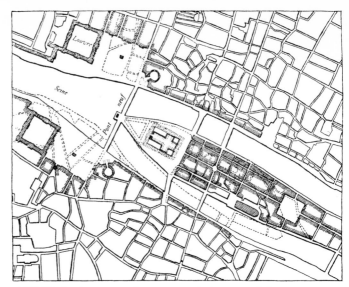

In Paris they were just as much interested in open spaces as in London but these continued to be of a different type. They were statue *places*. Louis XIV or, as he was named on the monuments, Louis le Grand, had had his *places*. Louis XV, *le bien aimé,* must also have his. The object was not only to glorify the monarchy, but also to beautify the city and rid it of slums. The old districts, in which houses were crowded together and unsavoury, were always present like a bad conscience.

In 1748 a great competition was held for the design of a monument *place* for Louis XV. The many plans that were sent in were reproduced in a large volume of engravings, published in 1765. But long before that year they had been spread all over Europe by newspapers and had been studied and copied even so far away as Denmark. The author of the stately work, Patte, had entered all the proposals on a map of Paris so that it resembled a city of royal *places*. And the proposals were by no means modest ones. One competitor sub-mitted a plan for a new Louvre on the left bank of the Seine, duplicating that on the right bank, and with the entire western end of the Isle de la Cité turned into a monumental *place,* in keeping with great, new *places* on both banks. Some pro-posed the destruction of large numbers of houses to make way for circular, quadrangular or octagonal *places*. There was also a design for a complete system of squares, three monumental market-places connected with each other by arcades. These

Patte: Monumens érigés à la gloire de Louis XV, 1765.

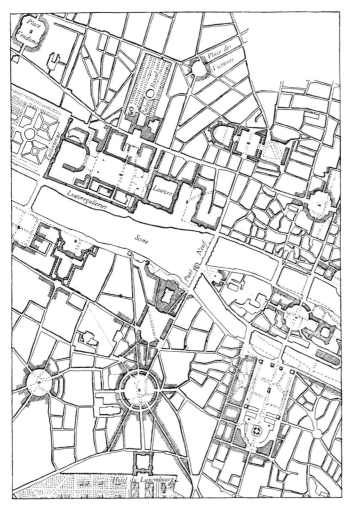

◄ *Proposal for a group of three monumental market-places connected by an arcade.*

Proposals for monumental squares in Paris in honour of Louis XV; results of a competition, 1748 — published 1765 — and never carried out. At top are seen two squares from Louis XIV' time: Place Vendôme and Place des Victoires. Scale 1 : 20.000. North upward.

many projects, however, did not lead to any slum clearance of the old districts. Instead, unbuilt land in front of the Tuileries was chosen as the site of the new *place,* bordered on one side by the Seine, on two others by rows of trees, and on the fourth side by new monumental buildings. In the centre a colossal equestrian statue of Louis XV was raised — now, long since vanished and replaced by a large obelisk.

This square is shown on the drawing, p. 167.

In the 18th century London continued to spread out, adding new residential sections around open squares. The landlords were the great landowners who were not used to selling their property but only to leasing it out on long term. This had been the custom since the Middle Ages and it had been a good one for agriculture. Now, the same system was continued after

113

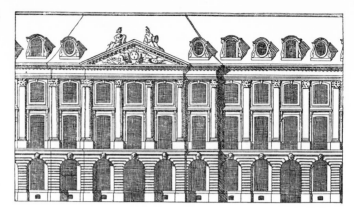

*Section of façade, Place Ven-
dôme, Paris. Scale 1 : 500.*

the property had become urban. The realisation of the appreciation of ground values took place only at long intervals, when
a tenancy, which might run for 99 years, had terminated. But
the owner could afford to wait. In London, which was a commercial city and where it was now possible to build as far
out as one wished, speculators thought in terms of *building*
speculation rather than *land* speculation, which are two very
different things. Money was invested in firms of enterprising
builders, and returns came as soon as the houses were finished
and sold. The money was used to *produce* something, and the
investor was not interested in building as many houses as possible on a piece of land, but only in building houses that were
as attractive as possible. And as it was attractive to live in a
house facing an open square, squares were naturally laid out.
When a district was no longer fashionable, the original residents moved to a new one, lying further out, which beckoned
with modern houses, larger open spaces and gardens.

The monumental *places* of continental cities, on the one
hand, and London's squares, on the other, were very different. The monumental *places* were great Baroque creations in
which the house façades were of paramount importance and
that which lay behind them quite unimportant. In the Place
Vendôme, as already noted, there was no connection between
the subdivisions on the façades surrounding the *place* and the
courtyards and rooms of the buildings behind them. (See
p. 108). The Baroque *place* was entirely dramatic in conception, forming an effective vista with entrance, approach and
climax. Such effects were not found in London, where all

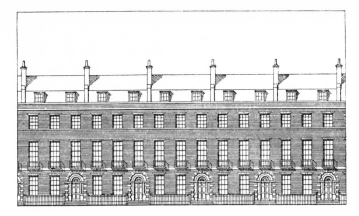

*Façades on Bedford Square,
London. Scale 1 : 500.*

four sides of the squares were generally the same. In the centre
there was usually a fenced-in garden to which all the families
living in the square had a key. The planting in them was
informal and trees were allowed to grow naturally, becoming
well formed and large. They were mostly plane trees. Neither
Baroque nor Rococo found favour in these districts, where the
houses were simple, anonymous brick buildings, their façades
relieved only by sharply indented window-openings. In all the
houses heating was done by coal fires on open hearths, which
spread a layer of soot over the whole city. The houses became
black. It was discovered that there were only two things to do
about this. Either the brick walls could be covered with stucco
and then oil painted, washed every year, and painted again
when necessary; or you could make a virtue of necessity by
painting the houses black from the start and, to relieve the
gloom, draw up the brickwork joints with very fine white
lines and paint the window casings a very light colour.
This was done in many cases and the charming effect became
a characteristic London trait.

On each building lot there was only one house for one
family. It might be a very large household with many family
members and servants. In Paris there were usually many
families in each house. At the entrance there was (and still is)
a special Paris institution, *le concierge*. No one could enter or
leave without passing him. He knew every inhabitant of his
little kingdom on the other side of the entrance and saw to it
that they received their mail and anything else brought to the
door for them ...

115

Under the influence of Carlyle, Charles Dickens wrote a book in 1859 which was very different from all his other books. Instead of describing his own time, he produced an historical novel, "A tale of Two Cities". It has not the documentary interest of many of his other books and there is, undoubtedly, some exaggeration in his description of monarchical Paris as compared to free London. But with amazing power he conjured up the two cities in unforgettable visions. As a symbol of Paris stands the minute and harrowing description of a staircase leading up through a tall tenement house, a steep and foul shaft with the doors of innumerable flats opening on to it. It symbolized the Paris that was tightly constricted within closed boundaries and which had to grow vertically because it could not spread out. At the very top of this dismal winding staircase was the miserable room where the noble and unhappy Dr. Manette had been brought after his mysterious release from the Bastille where he had been a life prisoner. Later in the book he is brought to London by friends and there we see him, sitting under a plane tree in his garden in Soho, a district of lovely squares where many emigrants found refuge. It is the London of the open spaces, with its air of humanity and with its green trees and black houses.

Paris and London symbolized.

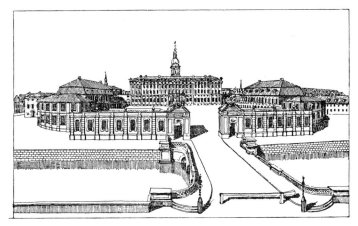

DANISH INTERMEZZO

The layout of Versailles, with the huge palace dominating the smaller town, became a model for court capitals all over Europe. Even the smallest German principality must have its majestic Baroque castle. In the phraseology of a later day, this has been explained as the desire of despotic princes to demonstrate their splendour and importance. And there is no doubt that many of those kings and dukes and bishops were fond of magnificent display. But there were also those who, though less interested in luxury, felt it *their duty* to live in accordance with the ideals of the time. A country with any pretensions to importance simply had to have its splendid palace representing the power and culture of the state. In terms of our money the total cost of the palace and parks of Versailles was no more than that of a modern warship, and who would deny that Versailles has been of more lasting value to the French nation than any dreadnought ever could be?

In Denmark we have an excellent example of palace building in the 18th century. Christian VI, who was king of Denmark and Norway, Duke of Slesvig and Holstein, etc. etc., and who reigned from 1730 to 1746, was a very modest and shy little man and the most dutiful servant of the State, devoting his time to working for his country and worshipping God. He considered it one of his duties to build palaces that would add to the glory of the absolute monarchy. Although he secured peace and prosperity for his country, he never became popular because he was both pious and tedious. Danish school

117

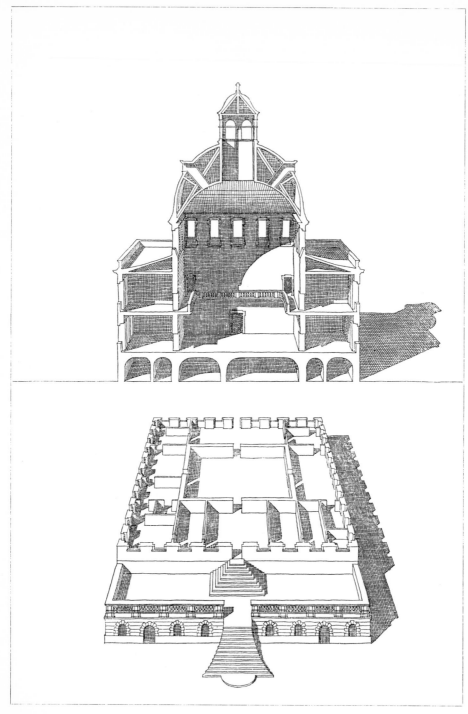

Fredensborg Castle as it originally appeared. Sectional drawing scaled to 1 : 500.

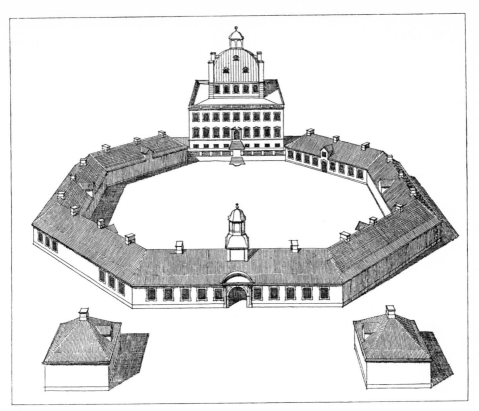

Fredensborg Castle as it originally appeared.

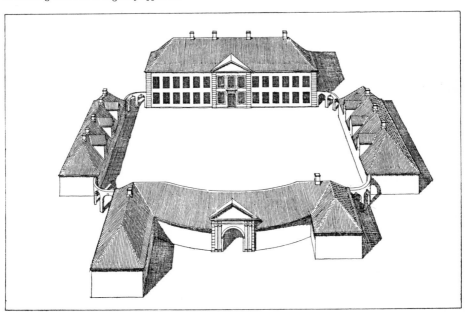

Roskilde Palace.

children are still taught that he squandered the country's wealth on the erection of unnecessary palaces, while other kings, who almost bankrupted Denmark by wars and great building schemes, are admired for their sense of beauty and their enterprise.

The palace of Christiansborg, in Copenhagen, which Christian VI built, would have been one of the great sights of Europe had it not been destroyed by fire in 1794. Not only was its architecture superb but it housed great treasures of European art, all of which disappeared in the flames. The few relics remaining, the stables and riding school and the colonnades surrounding the great forecourt, are splendid examples of Baroque architecture, comparable to similar structures at Schönbrunn in Vienna and Ludwigsburg near Stuttgart.

Christian VI carried out a great building programme: for his capital and seat of residence he built the monumental Christiansborg; in the small country town of Hørsholm, about 15 miles from the capital, he erected a vast summer residence in the woods; in the deer park some few miles north of Copenhagen he built a hunting lodge, "The Hermitage", a little gem of Baroque architecture. There, he and his queen could have their meals served on a table that was hoisted up to the dining-room on a lift, the meal arranged on it, so that they could dine in complete privacy in a beautiful room with a magnificent view over the woods and nearby Sound. On the coast he built a small palace, Sophienberg, as a retreat for the queen.

Those who believe that the architecture of a period is a true picture of the social conditions prevailing at the time, will have difficulty in fitting their theory to the vigorous and sumptuous Baroque built by this dull, pious man whose court was solemn and austere. His father, Frederik IV, had been a much more worldly monarch who had had many gallant adventures on his Grand Tour of Europe. After his return he built a summer residence, Fredensborg (1720-22), which shows influences from his visits to Italian villas and *Marly le Roy*. It is a strictly geometric structure with a high square-domed hall and an octagonal courtyard surrounded by low pavilions. The buildings erected by Christian VI, who was a skilful amateur architect, have a freer and more organic form. While the gay and sensual father had been a mathematically-

Roskilde Palace. The convex
stable wing seen from the
market place. Erected 1733.
Designed by Laurids Thurah.

minded architect, his sober and sedate son was a much more imaginative builder. This is very evident in the charming little "Roskilde Palace" which, though small and very modest compared to Christiansborg, shows the same virtuosity in the handling of the building masses. The convex wing facing the street meets the visitor with a high, tiled roof pierced by the pediment of the entrance portal, the whole composition reminiscent of a gate in a city wall. Inside the court the four wings appear as independent structures though they are skilfully linked together by archways at all four corners. There is something almost monastic about this quiet enclosure, formed by four simple Danish houses, and this atmosphere is heightened by the Gothic silhouette of the neighbouring cathedral, which rises above the horizontal roof-line of the buildings. It is a superb contrast — the many slender spires piercing the skies and the compact volume of the regular courtyard which seems to exercise a mild pressure on the plastic buildings surrounding it.

The architect's drawings for Christiansborg show how rich the details of that palace must have been. It became the model for all new houses of any pretensions in Copenhagen. An excellent example of one of these still exists in the buildings of the Asiatic Company in the town of Christianshavn just across the harbour from the capital. This building is like a great, solid block that has been enriched by the addition of more and more material. The façade rises to a semi-circular pediment above the cornice and the same *motif* is repeated in the boldly projecting mouldings over the windows of the second-storey. The two upper storeys are united by four gigantic pilasters which are carried up through the cornice, where they bend at right angles to follow its lines. Horizont-

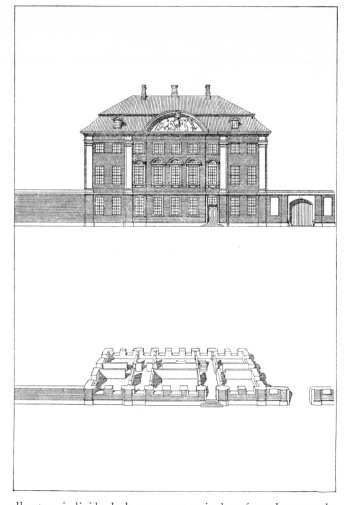

Typical Danish Baroque building with high vaulted roof and with all decoration superimposed on the solid block of the building.

The Asiatic Company's building, Christianshavn. Façade scaled to 1 : 500.   Erected 1738-39. Architect Philip de Lange.

Asiatic Company. Courtyard entrance.

ally, too, individual elements are united to form larger units of varying sizes, which skilfully break the monotony of a flat façade. The lovely portal which delights the eye on entering the courtyard uniting the twin buildings, probably demonstrates better than anything else this style in which the architecture is enhanced by the addition of more and more material to the original form. The central part of the façade stands out clearly from the rest of the building and from this, again, the richly ornamented entrance projects boldly while its pediment breaks through the string course above it, and is itself broken by magnificent sculptural ornaments consisting of scrolls, olive branches and conch shells. Everything is massive and virile, symmetrical and firm.

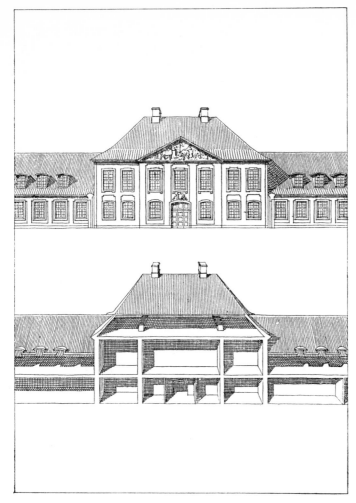

*Typical Danish Rococo build-
ing with concave roof-line
and recessed façade relief.*

*Main pavilion of the Royal
Frederik Hospital, Copen-
hagen. Erected 1752-54.
Architect Nicolai Eigtved.*

A Baroque house of this type is not at its best standing in
an ordinary street row; all four sides must be visible, disclos-
ing its great form. When it was necessary to build these houses
in rows, they asserted themselves in another way. Above the
cornice a walled dormer shot up, standing out boldly from
the sloping roof, so that, from the side, it could still be seen
that the house had a solid body. Another distinguishing feature
of Copenhagen's Baroque houses was their brilliant colouring.
They were often painted in several colours or contrasts were
obtained by a combination of rugged, plastered ashlar and
red brick. It has become customary to consider *Baroque*
architecture a deterioration of the "pure" style of the Renaissance, while *Rococo,* which followed, has long been regarded as

Baroque houses in street row, Copenhagen. Here the solidity and bulk typical of the Baroque is intimated by walled dormers rising above the crowning cornices. Scale 1 : 500.

Baroque chair.

Rococo chair.

out-and-out perversion. It is so easy to explain Rococo art as a result of the general decadence of the 18th century, Why, Rococo ornament is not even symmetrical! According to this conception, the many sinuous curls and scrolls of the Rococo decoration of the time of the Danish king, Frederik V (1746— 66), can be regarded as a graphic illustration of the crooked path trodden by that merry monarch. Critics have been so blinded by empty theory that they have not been able to *see* what Rococo really is, regarding it simply as a style of ornament. And yet, the truth is that — in Denmark, at any rate — the introduction of Rococo signalized an entirely new conception of architecture. People had become surfeited with the richness af Baroque and were ready for a more rational and unrestrained style. And then, at the psychological moment, Rococo appeared. While the Baroque mode of expression consisted in adding more and more material to the surface of an already massive form — it might be called the *addition* method — the new style introduced a period in which *subtraction* was the rule. The Rococo architect preferred to relieve his façades by recessing, rather than projection, when it could be done without weakening construction. Houses were now to appear light and elegant instead of massive and heavy; whatever was essential and pleasant was also desirable, but all redundancy was scorned. It is characteristic of the two periods that while the Baroque chair was large and highbacked, investing the occupant with even more dignity than his splendid costume and great wig gave him, the Rococo chair was small and light, formed like a piece of fine sculpture, pleasant to the touch, and better adapted for comfortable relaxation than a stiff and haughty posture.

124

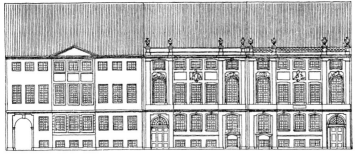

Rococo houses in street row, Amalie Street, Copenhagen, uniform in height; in only one case a pediment rises above the crowning cornice Scale 1 : 500.

Rococo is far from being a licentious style. It denotes a discriminating taste, intelligent reserve and calm rationalism. Rococo artists were interested in what things were used for, in their *function*. They employed human proportions in their work. They originated panel-clad walls, which made the heating of rooms easier and could conceal built-in cupboards. They rejected brilliant, florid colours for white and grey, which brought out the delicate stucco ornament of the rooms. The proportions of their buildings might be geometrically worked out down to the last detail, but they happily avoided lifeless and uninspiring formalism. When ornament was used, it had the flowing lines of conch shells, swags and festoons, freely growing out of the fine, white plaster and giving life and plasticity to the strict regularity of the room.

This Rococo style, so expressive of good taste, has nowhere left lovelier traces than in Copenhagen. It was brought to the capital by one of the few Danish architectural geniuses, Nicolai Eigtved (1701—54), who had studied the style and built in it during a long sojourn abroad. On his return, competition immediately arose between the Baroque architects of the city and the envoy of the new style. Christian VI's great castle was under construction and in the competitions for the work still to be done, Eigtved was continually the victor. He designed the marble bridge leading to the courtyard and the two pavilions which form the entrance to the riding school and was also responsible for much of the work in the interior of the royal residence. More and more work was entrusted to him, both large and small undertakings. But his greatest achievement was the planning of an entire new quarter with all its buildings, the Amalienborg district in Copenhagen, to-day the site of the royal residence.

The concentration of power in the hands of despotic kings made possible an artificial development of cities totally unlike the natural growth of medieval towns. By a stroke of the king's pen, new cities, or new enclaves within old cities, could be made to spring up over night, as it were. In contrast, the medieval city developed naturally, according to the needs of the economic life of the town. Now, the state could decide *what* commerce there should be and *where* it was to be carried on. Towns could be laid out where there were no natural conditions for a town. Great wealth could be created for the privileged few, but nothing could be done to save the many from complete dependence and abject poverty.

All this led to the cultural flowering of a small, privileged class and the flourishing of art, science and philosophy. The social problems of the day were by no means ignored but no one seemed able to find a solution to them. Philosophers and writers, who criticized conditions, received financial support from the courts, where their works were read and they, themselves, received with all honours. The theories which were to form the theoretical basis of future revolutions, were first put forward in the literary salons of the nobility of the 18th century. The members of these select coteries discussed the creation of ideal states and ideal cities, but were able to realize them for only a small, privileged group of society. These fortunate few lived in the most beautiful surroundings imaginable, where nothing was lacking for their comfort and well-being. In this framework, which bore the impress of great refinement of taste, they discussed social problems or, when sentimentally inclined, romanticized about the simple and virtuous lives of the deserving poor.

On the occasion of the 300th anniversary of the House of Oldenborg, in 1749, King Frederik V decided to bestow on his subjects the very large area comprising the park of one of the royal palaces, which had been destroyed by fire, and the adjoining drill ground. Official notice was published offering prospective builders sites on this land which was, according to the proclamation, "a very advantageous neighbourhood for the negotiators due to the proximity of the harbour and the Customs House, which will greatly contribute to the facilitation and advancement of commerce".

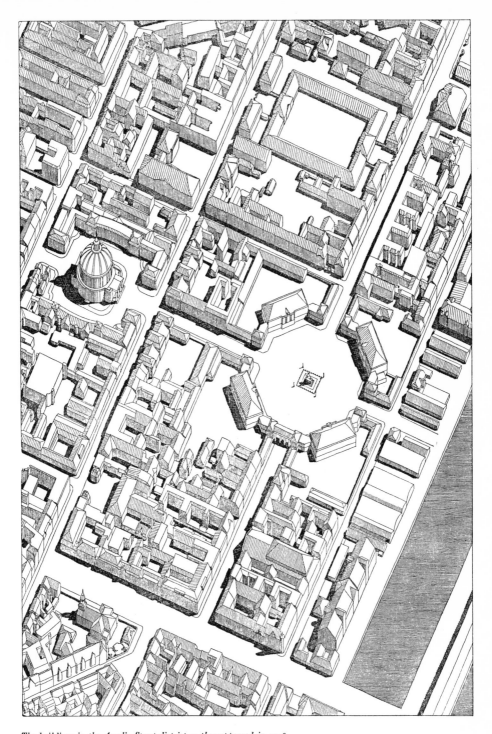

The buildings in the Amalie Street district as they appeared in 1948.

It would seem clear, from this, that the king's intention had been to create a commercial centre in connection with the harbour. Those who were willing to erect houses would receive the land as a freehold and be given thirty years' exemption from military billeting. Timber merchants, who had their yards in the neigbourhood, were to have preference in the choice of sites. But if they did not immediately send in their applications, anyone, of whatever class of society, had permission to apply and the applicants would then be allowed to choose sites in the order in which their applications had been received. They would at once take ownership, the only conditions being that they were to build within five years and, in every detail, adhere to the plans approved by the king. "Uniformity must be observed in every respect" and all buildings facing the street were to be constructed of brick with windows in horizontal rows.

But from the very first something more than an ordinary commercial centre must have been contemplated. On the original plan, which no longer exists, a great central *place* had been sketched in and the king expressly says that he will reserve the grounds on which "the four palaces are to be located which will form the central *place*".

It is not difficult to guess from where the architect, Eigtved, had got the idea for this great monument plaza. A competition had been held the year before in Paris for a *place* built around a statue of Louis XV. Among the projects sent in had been a design for an octagonal plaza on an axis running at right angles to the Seine. But though Amalienborg Place may have been inspired by Paris, Eigtved's plan is entirely original. It is not, as is true of similar French projects, simply a number of building-façades of uniform height, hiding what lies behind. It is a deliberately concieved composition of building units of varying sizes and shapes which, together, form a rhythmic whole. There was nothing nebulous in Eigtved's composition. The corners were held fast by substantial building blocks, rising above the others in the street. On either side of the streets approaching the great plaza he planned rows of plain, uniform houses to emphasize the splendour of the Amalienborg Place, with its four flanking palaces and central monument. Here, too, the corners are clearly marked by two-storey pavilions rising at

See p. 112.

Not shown on the plans pp. 112-113.

*Vista from Amalienborg Place
as originally planned by the
architect. Scale 1 : 1000. In
foreground two of the Amalienborg palaces, behind them
in outline twin houses at end
of Frederik's Street, rising
above them the Marble Church
as originally designed by
Eigtved.*

the end of the one-storey "galleries" adjoining the palaces and
uniting them with the pavilions. The result is the unique
motif of four palaces, each one an individual unit consisting of
a central building flanked by two pavilions, which together
form the larger unit of the octagonal *place*. At the opposite
end of Frederik's Street, running west from the *place,* this
three-part composition of house and pavilions is repeated in the
two fine houses on the corners. Unhappily, the magnificent
Marble Church with its colossal dome and flanking towers —
again the triple composition — which was to have closed this
vista from the plaza through Frederik's Street, was never
completed as planned by Eigtved. Therefore, the dramatic
crescendo he had visualized, beginning with the two palace
pavilions at the Frederik's Street corner of the *place,* and rising
to the taller buildings af the opposite end of the street, to end
with the mighty dome of the Marble Church — high, higher,

129

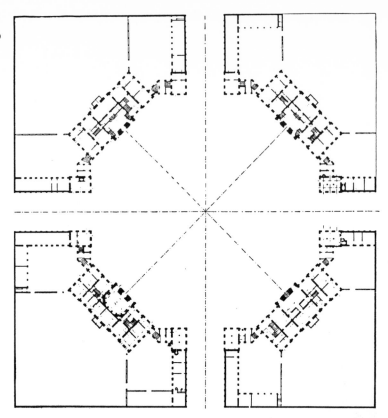

*Amalienborg Place, Copen-
hagen, ground floor plan.
Scale 1 : 2000. Building commenced 1749 after plans of
Nicolai Eigtved. (After un-
published part of Thurah's
Vitruvius.) Lower left-hand
corner now Christian VII's
Palace. (Compare p. 131).*

highest — was never fully realized. This same crescendo is also
apparent in the individual buildings but was especially marked
in the original church design where the eye would naturally
have ranged from the low entrance storey, 20-foot high, the
40-foot second-storey, the 80-foot cylinder to the dome rising
160 feet to the cross.

The new quarter grew out of a royal garden and there is
still a reminiscence of a detached villa in the composition
of the Amalienborg palaces with their sidewings and pavilions.
Originally there was an entrance in the centre of the façade
of each one, which led directly from the plaza into a kind of
garden room. In the building which later became the residence
of Christian VII, this was a niche-shaped room, resembling a
patio, with a tiled floor almost on a level with the pavement
outside, and with stone columns at intervals round the wall.
From it, steps led up to the living rooms on the ground floor.
The grand salon of the second-storey is marked on the façade
by a slightly projecting loggia of columns in pairs and there

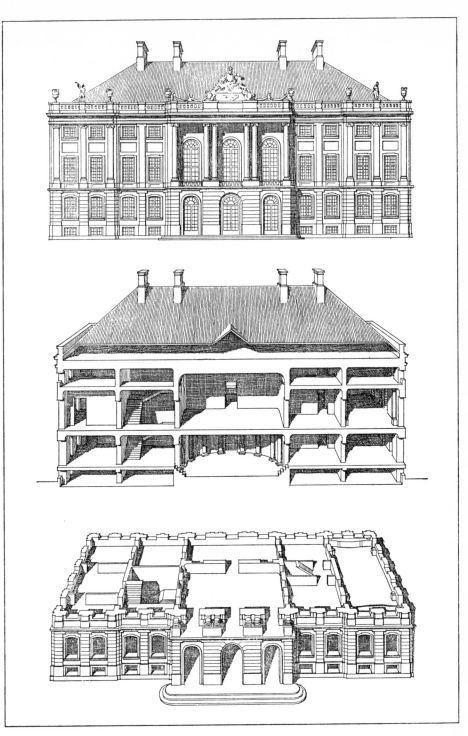

Amalienborg, Copenhagen. Christian VII's Palace. Façade scaled to 1 : 500.

are also shallow projecting end bays on this palace. In fact, the entire building is clearly divided up in bays. The central bay has three broad and high windows of equal size, each one seen between a pair of colums. On either side of this, the recessed bays have two smaller windows, each, as have also the projecting end bays. These windows are all repeated in the rear wall. Along both sides of the building are five of the smaller windows. If lines were drawn from the centre of each window to the corresponding window opposite, it would be discovered that all doors and niches lie along them. This gives long vistas through the building and rooms of simple dimensions. They may be square or in a ratio of two to three, or one to two on plan. The four palaces are not absolutely uniform but they are all built along the same lines.

We cannot fail to admire the ability of the 18th century to build up an entire new quarter at one stroke. The plans of the Amalienborg district were first laid in 1749 and when Eigtved died in 1754 the whole of the extensive quarter with its beautiful palaces, a handsome hospital, and its many fine houses, was entirely laid out and many of the buildings completed. This was possible only because Eigtved fully mastered his art. In all his undertakings he worked with dimensions and shapes with which he was entirely familiar. He was able to combine them to form extraordinary compositions like the really quite extravagant church project. But he could also use them for purely functional buildings, such as Frederik's Hospital, in which the dimensions of the long wards are based on the size of hospital beds, and the wards located to obtain the best light. And there is the warehouse of the Asiatic Company, down by the harbour, in which the hoisting lofts are the dominating *motif*. In all his works, small as well as great, Eigtved demonstrated that it is the architect's problem to join the various elements of a building together in a clear and convincing manner, and to group them into inherent units.

The Amalienborg quarter became a district of grey houses in contrast to the brightly coloured older sections of the city. Immediately after Eigtved's death a strong reaction to Rococo was evident. The new catchword was "pure classicism". But the streets of Copenhagen continued well into the 19th century to be of the type Eigtved had given to the capital.

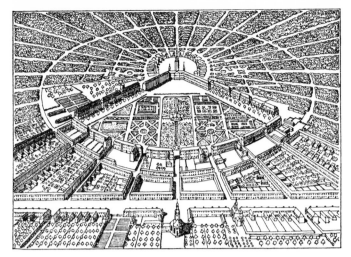

Karlsruhe, after a plan from the middle of the 18th century. The tower is seen marking the centre both of the star formed by the meeting of the forest roads and of the radial streets of the town. The tower stands in conjunction with the central block of the 3-winged castle. South of it are seen the parterre gardens and the city with the two "ring" streets. Further south Langestrasse and just below it, on the main axis, the Reformed Church.

NEO-CLASSICISM

Once upon a time there was a prince — thus begins the story of Karlsruhe. His name was Karl Wilhelm and he was a margrave. The country he ruled over was only a small one but — like all princes — he was a noble lord, beloved by all his subjects. His country, which was called Baden-Durlach, had been devastated by war, his castle plundered and burned, and he longed only for peace and happiness.

When the war was over he did not wish to burden his impoverished people with the cost of rebuilding the great castle and fortifications of the residential city. He decided instead to live close to nature in the neighbouring forest where he would build a simple dwelling of wood. There, peace would be disturbed only by the merry notes of hunting horns ... And so, where the roads of the forest met to form a giant star, he built himself a tower.

Karlsruhe founded in 1715.

Two longs wings gradually grew out from this tower, with audience chambers, with a chapel, and with a play-house, all built of wood. He called the place *Karlsruhe,* which means Karl's Rest. The entire court of the little country moved out to this unfortified hunting chateau and, in the midst of the forest, a town sprang up in a semi-circle round the castle. The margrave, himself, drew the plans for the city and when he went up in the tower he could look down on his town just as a gaoler can see into every corner of his prison yard, peer down all the streets and into all the roads of the forest.

133

This it not a fairy tale but a true and just description of how a city might come into being at the beginning of the 18th century.

The next chapter of our story tells of the metamorphosis of the town under the hands of a very enlightened prince called Karl Friedrich, who reigned from 1748 to 1811. In 1748 the castle was rebuilt of brick and stone and a circular court street laid out in Rococo style, arcaded all the way. Directly in line with the castle, on an axis at right angles to the main highway, *Langestrasse,* a church was erected. Karl Friedrich was a true disciple of the Age of Enlightenment. He abolished serfdom and gathered philosophers and poets around him at court.

And Baden prospered and the city grew. Soon it was so crowded that it became necessary to build on the other side of *Langestrasse.* There where the church stood, the town's market-place was now to be located. In 1787 the Italian, Peddetti, drew up plans for it, a real Baroque project. From *Langestrasse* there was to be access to a broad market-place and at the opposite end, where it narrowed into a street, he proposed the erection of two symmetrical domed churches with columned façades and towers. But his proposal was not carried out. It was the architect Friedrich Weinbrenner who left his

Below:
Karlsruhe 1834. North upward. Scale 1 : 20.000. At top the original Karlsruhe; south of Langestrasse, which terminates east and west in a classic gateway, is seen the new district laid out according to Weinbrenner's plans.

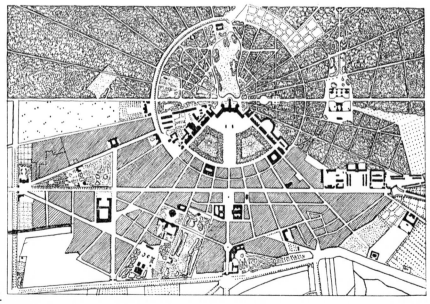

F. Weinbrenner's proposal for the regulating af Langestrasse in Karlsruhe, involving high arcades to be erected in front of all existing façades.

stamp on the new section of the city during the first decades
of the 19th century. As the fan-shaped formation of the first
building period did not easily lend itself to the new district on
the other side of *Langestrasse,* Weinbrenner drew up a new
geometric system of streets. The city was still without fortifications but its entrances were now marked by gateways which
were the starting-points of main thoroughfares. While the
circular street near the castle was lined with handsome,
uniform façades, the lengthy *Langestrasse* had a very irregular
frontage of high and low houses mixed together. Weinbrenner
proposed the erection of a uniform screen for all the houses,
consisting of arcades with arches as tall as the highest building,
systematically carried out on both sides of the long street.
While Baroque had striven for the interesting vista, Neo-
Classicism was first and foremost concerned with purity of
style; style so chaste as to be almost sterile. Classical columns,
square pillars and semi-circular arches meant purity of style
and insured classic beauty. Neither was this project, however,
carried out.

The market-place was now to be classically austere instead
of the vigorous Baroque proposed by Pedetti. A drawing made
by Weinbrenner in 1797 still exists. It shows a square immediately adjoining *Langestrasse.* In Neo-Classicism *places* were
always given simple, geometric forms. This one is surrounded
by one-storey buildings in what was then considered Greek
style, with arcades facing the square — like refined market-
halls. This forecourt, with a monument in the centre, opens
on to a larger rectangular *place.* Along both sides of it are

See: Arthur Valdenaire:
Friedrich Weinbrenner.
Karlsruhe, 1923.

135

shown porticoed temple façades, one leading into the cathedral, the other to the town hall. Here, too, there is a monument in the centre. Further along the main axis lies a circular *place*. Circles were guaranteed handsome, just as squares were, and could be employed where there were no awkward street-crossings. In a beautiful sketch Weinbrenner has shown how the whole project would appear. In the foreground we see the square with the Greek market-hall and behind it the pediment of the town hall. In the distant background an obelisk marks the centre of the circus. The Grecian market-halls were never built. But Weinbrenner did build the church and the town hall and many other buildings, both public and private. In the centre of the market-place a pyramid was erected.

He found intricate solutions to problems involving corner houses on circular *places*. He proposed plans for the zoning of buildings, with the tallest and finest grouped round the central axis and smaller ones located out toward the periphery. He made type drawings for dwelling houses. Weinbrenner left Karlsruhe a perfect example of a Biedermeier city with neat plastered buildings embellished with classical columns and pediments.

What happened in Karlsruhe was repeated in many European cities. The more voluptuous and organic forms of Baroque design gave way to the geometric and sterile Neo-Classic style. This was not only true of individual buildings but of town-planning on the whole.

There is on the Continent a tendency to present European art history as an uninterrupted sequence, a history of simple evolution from Renaissance to Baroque, from Baroque to Rococo, and from Rococo to Neo-Classicism. The pictures in many art collections, too, have been arranged according to the same theory so that museum visitors have only to pass from room to room in their numerical order to review our entire cultural development at a glance, so to speak. But the truth is much more complicated. It is a significant fact that English art is seldom included in such museums, and still less the art of China, though that alien culture strongly influenced European art in the 18th century.

There was not one country in Europe that had not been subject to influences from many quarters. The development

Amaliegade in Copenhagen. The houses in the foreground were built in the Rococo-period. Further down the street there are houses in the Neo-Classical style. The vista is closed by the Greek revival colonnade shown on page 140.

of art, therefore, cannot be looked on as a single trend, easily followed. It includes many trends, now meeting and mingling, now going their several ways. In provincial places such as Karlsruhe the various periods can be associated with the work of a few leading architects and, likewise, in Denmark it is possible to show that Rococo was the court style from 1735 to 1754, when Nicolai Eigtved died, and that it was superseded by a kind of new Classicism. But in 1747, when Eigtved built the Danish Royal Theatre in Rococo, Knobelsdorff's Neo-Classic opera house in Berlin was already four years old. And in England there had been an unbroken tradition of a classical Renaissance for generations. Ever since the days of Inigo Jones (1573—1653) there have been English architects who have built in a Palladian style. Houses can be found in England closely resembling Palladio's Villa Rotonda, but there are also interesting original works, such as the great house at Prior Park, built about 1735 (see p. 36) by the elder John Wood. The Woods, father and son, were the architects of the strictly classical part of Bath with its rectangular Queen's Square (1727) from which Gay Street (between 1750 and 1760) rises to the geometric perfection of the Circus (1754) and continues to the stately Royal Crescent (1767). At the same time that the Rococo style was celebrating its greatest triumphs in town-planning in Nancy (1753—1755) and Copenhagen (1750—54), this model city of squares and crescents was being laid out and adorned with colonnaded façades of the purest classicism.

See: Walter Ison: The Georgian Buildings of Bath 1700—1830. London. 1948.

137

Starting in 1766, the most superb classical town-planning was carried out in Great Britain when the New Town was laid out in Edinburgh. It was planned by James Craig and the Adam brothers were responsible for many of its new houses.

It is difficult to trace the influence this persistent Palladianism in England has had on the rest of Europe. Very few continental Europeans travelled to Great Britain to see buildings. But English architecture was known through illustrated books on the subject. Colin Campbell had published the great *Vitruvius Britannicus* (1715—1725) which purported to show the best of English architecture but which gave predominance to his own and his friends' work—in the Palladian manner. Through such books English architecture influenced European building just as contemporary books on English philosophical and social subjects won adherents among liberal-minded people on the Continent. It is significant that when Knobelsdorff, who had been in Italy from 1738 to 1739, desired to give his Berlin opera house a classical stamp, he procured the work of an *English* architect, Inigo Jones, containing illustrations of Palladio's buildings. His contemporaries found the opera house a perfect example of *Greek* architecture. Voltaire wrote to his niece: "It was like a Greek temple in which the work of barbarians was performed." (Life at the court of Frederick the Great *was* barbaric in the eyes of a visitor from Paris.)

There existed at the time only vague ideas of what Greek architecture really was like. And while architects in countries where Baroque and Rococo had flourished turned back to Palladio to attain a purer, a *more* classic style, the English felt that Palladio's style, which they knew by heart, was not classical *enough*. James Adam wrote in his diary in the Autumn of 1760 at Vicenza: ". . . to see the different buildings of Palladio with which this city abounds, and of which I am no admirer." His brother, Robert Adam, had measured the ruins of Diocletian's palace at Spalato in Dalmatia in 1757. (Later the Adam brothers were to return to Palladio's style and would be responsible for many more so-called "Palladian windows" than Palladio, himself, had built in Italy.) At this period many English architects made measurements of classic architecture in Greece which earlier had been a *terra incognita*. Of special importance was one such journey made by James

See: The Age of Adam by James Lees-Milne. London, 1947, page 57.

See: Apollo or Baboon by Nikolaus Pevsner and S. Lang. Architectural Review. Dec. 1948. p. 271.

Stuart (1713—1788) and Nicholas Revett (1721—1804), who were sent out by the *Society of Dillettanti*. Their scale drawings, which were published in two volumes in 1762 and 1768 proved that the correct Greek columns were very different from the hitherto authorized orders. The older generation found that the Greek columns of the measurements were barbaric; the younger generation were enthusiastic about them and prided themselves on being as archeologically correct as possible.

Neo-Classicism became an architectural programme, so to speak, in protest against the "turgidity" of Baroque, claiming simplicity and purity for itself. Its recipe was quite simple: the main forms were based on a pattern of simple geometric figures, the details were to be pure Greek and the surroundings formed according to the ideals of English landscape gardening. Its lesser works are a mechanical compilation of these elements but in some of its great monuments the architects succeeded in creating what Robert Adam called "a greater movement". He explains this in the following words: "Movement is meant to express the rise and fall, the advance and recess with other diversity of form, in the different parts of a building, so as to add greatly to the picturesqueness of the composition." The effect of a single, delicately contrived detail was often enhanced by a background of purely abstract form, as when Claude-Nicolas Ledoux (1756—1806) designed spherical and pyramidal edifices with a single columned portico. The predilections of the period for geometric forms and for pastoral idylls are combined in C. F. Hansen's circular country house outside Altona.

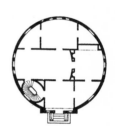

C. F. Hansen (1756—1845): country house near Altona. Scale 1 : 500.

See: Claude-Nicolas Ledoux, by Marcel Raval, Paris, 1945.

Sofienholm outside Copenhagen designed by the French architect Joseph-Jacques Ramée (1764-1842) who worked first for l'ancien regime, then for the Revolution; from 1790 for rich merchants in Hamburg and Copenhagen; in the U. S. A. 1811-16 he designed Union College in Schenectady (1812). 1823 found him back in Paris.

Colonnade connecting two of Amalienborg's four palaces at the end of Amalie Street in Copenhagen. Façade reproduced on a scale of c. 1:500. After the partial destruction of Christiansborg Castle by fire in 1794 the king acquired the Amalienborg palaces (still the royal residence) which were originally built for private owners. As any one of the palaces was too small for a royal residence, the architect Harsdorff was engaged to unite two of them without interfering with the view of Sally's equestrian statue from Amalie Street.

All this awakened an interest in columns for their own sake. Quite a number of the buildings of the period gave the impression of having been built as an excuse to employ the adored columns. When Goethe—who admired Palladio just as much as James Adam despised him—visited Vicenza in 1786, he wrote in his diary on September 19th: "The greatest problem which this man, as all modern architects, had to struggle with was how to employ the orders of columns on private houses, because to combine columns and walls will always be a contradiction." Some architects overcame this contradiction by forming their buildings like great colonnades. In Paris, Ange-Jacques Gabriel (1782) built a row of magnificent façades facing the *Place Louis XV* with a colonnade across the fronts. But here Renaissance columns were still employed. When the Danish royal family purchased the Amalienborg Palaces for

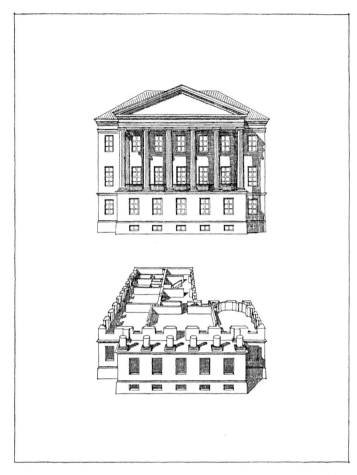

The Erichsen town house (now the Handels Bank) in Copenhagen near the Kings's New Square. Façade scale c.1:500. Erected according to plans drawn by Caspar Harsdorff, 1799. The composition is reminiscent of Palladio's villas, with a great pillared loggia. (Compare Villa Piovene, p. 73). The six Ionic columns are very accurate copies of Greek originals, familiar to Harsdorff from the measurements published at the time in books on research amon Greek antiquities.

the royal residence after Christiansborg had been destroyed by fire in 1794, the architect C. F. Harsdorff (1735—1799) was engaged to link two of them together across an intervening street. He was delighted to be able to carry out the work with Ionic columns in the Greek form as he knew it from Stuart and Revett's drawings. Later he built a private house in Copenhagen (Erichsen's Palais) which is formed in the Palladian manner but all details are pure Greek.

The French Revolution did not lead to a revolution in style but carried on from where the monarchy had left off. In 1793 an arts' commission was set up in Paris, *Commission temporaire d'artistes,* composed of painters, architects and engineers. They were to propose a comprehensive plan not only for the new sections of the city but for the regulation of the whole of Paris. It was to include suggestions for new traffic arteries, plans for the beautification of the city, and slum clearance. It is interesting to note that the work was based on a masterly survey of Paris begun in 1773, under Louis XVI, and was completed during the reign of Napoleon. Thus the work went steadily forward despite all political cataclysms.

The long *Rue de Rivoli,* carried out by Napoleon from the *Place de la Concorde* to the Louvre, is characteristic of the style of the period, which we call the Empire style. Today, its classicism reminds us of Hitler's and Stalin's architecture. But while the newer dictators forced a classicism to flourish where they had found a modernism, Napoleon converted the existing tendencies in art to his own use.

Napoleon was, in all respects, a disciple of the 18th century. The Empire style was not created by his regime—on the contrary, it can be maintained that the existing style led to the Empire. The curtain had fallen on the first acts which had recalled ancient Rome: first the Republic and then the Consulate. Napoleon, who was a student of history, knew that the next act called for a Caesar. Politically it was important for him to consolidate his position, to make it legitimate. In the year 1802 he had written to Louis XVIII in his exile, suggesting legal abdication in favour of Napoleon. When this was refused he perceived that it was the wrong thing to attempt to compete with the Bourbons. They were completely out of date, now. The classical style was *en vogue,* it was time for the Roman emperor to appear. In 1804 he ordered a coronation robe reminiscent of a toga. At his request the pope arrived from Rome, itself, and Napoleon, appropriately clad, had only to take the stage where the supporting cast awaited his coming. Everything was to bear the stamp of the new empire as quickly as possible. Just as Caesar had had his Egyptian adventures, Napoleon had his memories of Africa. Roman and Egyptian attributes were reproduced in great quantities and applied to buildings, furniture and household equipment. Soon they were pouring out of the factories. Allegorical trappings became cheap. Sculptors made busts and statues of the emperor which more and more came to resemble Augustus, almost to the point of misidentification. Paris was to be a new Rome where victories would be celebrated by the erection of triumphal columns and arches.

In 1798 General Bonaparte had said: "If I were master in France I would not only make Paris the most beautiful city in existance or that ever has existed but the most beautiful there ever could be." The time had now come to carry out this programme. He inaugurated great works just as Sixtus V had done in his day in Rome. He provided the city with a better water supply, built market halls and bridges, opened up new thoroughfares and raised monuments to honour his victories and his regime.

Compare p. 48.

He had a good working basis in the Paris of the Bourbons. The Louvre was completed and the Tuileries enlarged by the addition of a long gallery matching the one built by Catherine de Medici (p. 56). He raised triumphal arches as a symbol of the emperor who went from victory to victory. In the great courtyard of the Tuileries he erected a regular Roman *porta triumphalis* with triple arches, in 1806. When the long wing of that palace was destroyed by fire in 1871, this *Arc de Triomphe du Carrousel* remained standing, marking the starting-point of that long axis, the *Champs Elysées*. And, of course, the terminal of those Elysian Fields could only be, in Napoleon's world, another arch of triumph. This great vista, which took its beginning when Catherine de Medici laid the foundation of the Tuileries outside the wall of Paris in 1564, advanced another step when the Tuileries' garden came under Le Nôtre's masterly hand and the long avenue was laid out, in 1664, and neared its goal when the *Place de la Concorde* was constructed a century later, was now to be completed and given its *raison d'être* by the erection of that great triumphal arch on the summit of the distant hill, a colossal monument to Napoleon's victories (finally completed under Louis Philippe in 1836).

See illustration p. 167.

The houses, like the Empire interiors and furniture, were designed by Napoleon's architects, Percier and Fontaine. They had studied classical architecture, as well as Renaissance and Baroque, in Italy. The results of their studies were published in a work on Roman palaces and houses. All buildings are depicted in the most delicate fine-lined drawings. In strong contrast to architectural engravings of the Baroque period, there is not the slightest hint of the texture of materials, or even shadows. All buildings look strangely alike in their attenuated versions. Their own architecture, too, as would be expected, turned out to be meagre interpretations of the Roman prototypes. All ornament was alike, whether carried out in marble, wood, bronze, or porcelain. But it was all delicate and decorous, which was the effect Napoleon—greatly handicapped by his family—tried so hard to give to his entire reign. This fragile classicism could be adapted without any great changes to suit the most unmitigated bourgeois taste, such as, for example, the German Biedermeier style.

During the continental blockade there was no communication between France and England but the difference in style was, nevertheless, slight. In Great Britain there was also a somewhat mechanical classicism. Regent Street was broken through in 1812 and a great number of houses built in it with columns and stucco ornament taken from catalogues of classical details. John Nash (1752—1835) was not too critical; his forte was the financing of these impressive undertakings and the grouping of building masses along great lines. But there were others who delved deeply into the study of the antique. St. Pancras Church, built by W. and H. W. Inwood in 1819—22, is composed of the most accurately reproduced Greek details. It has two complete caryatid halls where the Erechtheion had to be satisfied with only one.

But when the architect had become a loyal copyist, who directly transposed great sections of an antique Greek temple to a modern Christian church, there were no longer any limits to how a building might be pieced together. The age of eclecticism had begun.

See: John Summerson. Georgian London, 1945 page 160 —173.

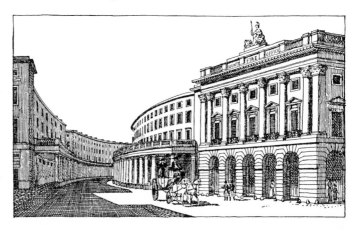

"The Quadrant", Regent Street, London, laid out in 1812. The sidewalks are carried out as curved arcades. The house façades were embellished with stucco ornament and oil painted. To-day the street is entirely different.

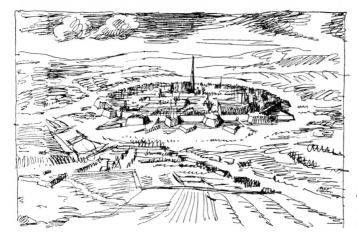

Vienna, the fortified city of the seventeenth century surrounded by a broad belt of open land.

THE BANLIEUES

At a time when Berlin was only a small colonial town in remote and barbaric Prussia, Vienna was the centre of Germanic culture with antecedents going all the way back to the Roman Empire. Like Paris and London, Vienna grew up around what had originally been a Roman garrison town. It had already attained importance in ancient times. Marcus Aurelius is believed to have died there in the year 180 A. D.

When the Turks overran Europe in the 16th century their advance was stopped at the gates of Vienna in 1529. The city was besieged but withstood the pressure. After three fruitless weeks the Turks retired and Vienna stood forth among the capitals of Europe as the great Germanic city that had hindered the Asiatic hordes from flooding the Continent—a border town and a great cultural centre at one and the same time. It was the home of the Habsburgs and the capital of the Holy Roman Empire—a political and cultural factor of quite different stamp than the German Empire at the end of the 19th century. It was a cosmopolitan city with an international culture.

The town walls were repeatedly augmented until Vienna lay safely within a strong ring of fortifications. It proved to have been necessary for the town was once more besieged by the Turks—in 1683. But after an attack on their long line of communications they were forced to withdraw and the creation of an alliance against the Ottoman Empire averted

145

the danger for all time. The Turks left behind two things which were to have a share in giving Vienna its special flavour—the café and the lilacs, both of which have since spread all over Europe.

Old engravings of Vienna show us a typical fortified town with a polygonal rampart reinforced with many bastions and moats. Outside the wall was a wide stretch of non-building land, a 600 ft. broad ring. Beyond that, widespread suburbs grew up. In the 17th century they were still villages containing small houses only. But soon they developed into regular urban districts. The Viennese aristocracy, not satisfied with their cramped dwellings in the old town, began to build great houses with magnificent gardens outside the walls. In 1704 the construction of outer defences was started for the protection of the suburbs. Vienna now consisted of two distinctly separated parts: innermost, the congested *Altstadt* with narrow streets, tall houses, great old churches, the palaces of the aristocracy, and *Hofburg,* the kaiser's residence; and separated from it by a broad belt of defence works and open land lay outer Vienna in the form of extensive suburbs with gardens and spreading trees.

When Napoleon occupied the city in 1809 he destroyed the bastions of the fortifications. From then on, Vienna was an "open" city, in the military sense, but for half a century the bastion ruins were allowed to lie where they had fallen, hindering the free expansion of the town. Not until 1857 was the decision taken to level the walls and incorporate the fortification terrain in the town plan. His "Imperial Royal Apostolic Majesty" proclaimed his desire to have work on the expansion of the old town started at once, particularly with a view to joining the two parts of the city and to the regulation and beautification of the residential city and imperial capital.

A detailed building programme was set up. A part of the area was to be parcelled out and sold as building sites. The money thus obtained was to form a building fund for the financing of the rest of the plan and the erection of a number of large public buildings. A public competition was opened the same year. In the building programme it had been laid down that the public edifices were, as far as possible, to stand alone,

Peterskirche in the old part of Vienna.

facing boulevards or squares. Therefore, all seven prize-win-
ners showed imposing structures, projected to stand completely
alone, free on all four sides, like building models with no
relation to their surroundings. This was in sharp contrast to
conditions in the old town where streets and squares formed
picturesque enclosures lined with rows of narrow houses.

The building programme was carried out with some modi-
fications during the following decades. A very broad boulevard
was laid out around the heart of the city, the so-called "Vienna
Ring", consisting of five rectilineal sections. The unbuilt areas
outside "the Ring" were sub-divided into rectangular blocks
and straight streets. Thus the new districts were made up
entirely of uniform building blocks except at the corners,
which would not come out right. The streets had no face;
they were simply voids, empty spaces between the cubic blocks,
not pleasant outdoor rooms as in old Vienna. In this way large
areas were added to Vienna in between the two older sections
and full advantage was taken of the opportunity offered to
locate the many public buildings the metropolis required near
the centre of the town. The result was a string of architectural
pearls—not genuine pearls but a heterogeneous collection of
imitations. One of the triangular open spaces was adorned
with a Neo-Gothic church hidden among lilac bushes and trees.
Gothic, too, was the new town hall, red brick Gothic like
that of old Lübeck, but magnified by a mechanical repetition
of arches and towers to the point of monstrosity. The *Burg*
Theatre, just opposite the town hall, was, on the other hand,
given Renaissance dress, as was also the stock exchange. The
finest of the lot was the parliament building, erected between
1874 and 1884 according to the design of the Danish architect Theophilus Hansen (1813—1891), an imposing edifice
in the Greek style, an allusion to the democratic institutions
of ancient Greece. The building, with its façade of many
accurately contrived Corinthian columns, is more Grecian in
detail than in lay-out and planning. It is dominated by an
enormous ramp leading up to the temple-like central portico.
The eclectic architecture of this man, who had both studied
and built in Athens, was to leave its stamp on the new Vienna,
not only in the form of imposing public buildings but also
in great blocks of flats of a lavish Renaissance design.

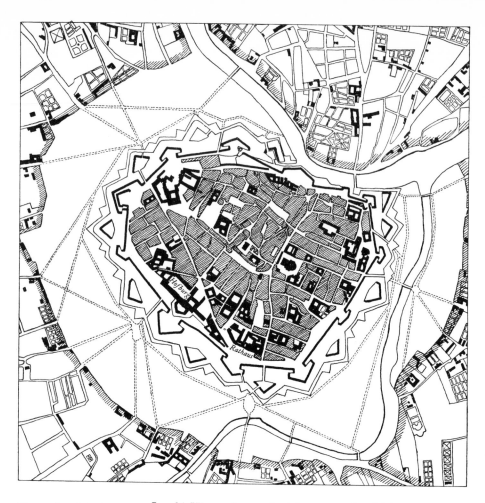

Vienna, Altstadt, in the 18th century. Scale 1:20.000. North upward.

In old Vienna houses had been growing higher and higher for some centuries. When the *Altstadt* could no longer expand in space, new storeys had been added when necessary to originally quite modest dwellings until they ended by being eight storeys high. For the new districts flats were planned in monumental blocks, regular in design and with streets on all four sides. They were projected as high as the highest buildings in the old town but with fewer storeys, as rooms were to be large and lofty. The new buildings did not have the organic appearance of the older ones which so manifestly revealed the development of centuries. This was drawing-board architecture which could stand ready for occupancy a year after the first stroke of the design had been put on paper. To relieve the chess-board regularity of the buildings the façades were

148

Vienna, Altstadt and the "Ring" at the end of the 19th century. Scale 1 : 20.000. North upward.

While Theophilus Hansen was leaving his stamp on Vienna, his brother, Christian Hansen (1803—88), was work-

*The City Hospital in Copen-
hagen before the walls fell.
After an old picture.*

ing on a "Ring" district in Copenhagen for which he designed
the great city hospital, *Kommunehospitalet* (1859—63), an extremely sober complex of buildings, monumental in conception,
modest in detail, and of very durable material: walls of yellow
and red brick, laid in stripes, with no projecting parts. The
entire spirit of the small Danish capital was very different
from that of Vienna but there were some of the same problems
to cope with. Copenhagen, like Vienna, was confined within
a polygonal rampart that had not been expanded since the
beginning of the 17th century despite the fact that the population had since grown five times as large. Here, too, there
was a broad, open area outside the walls where building had
been prohibited as a defence measure. And also in Copenhagen
the question of how to link the old town with the suburbs,
now that the walls were to be moved further out, was one of
the great problems of the century.

This old Copenhagen behind the ramparts with their cherry
tree lined walks has been romanticized by later writers into
a most charming community. But the truth is that in the old
town, where Hans Andersen, Søren Kierkegaard, N. F. S.
Grundtvig, and a host of other literary figures of lesser renown,
could be seen daily strolling along the main thoroughfare,
conditions behind the façades were as bad as they could be.
Not only were houses squeezed together as tightly as possible
because the city was cut off from expansion, but the sanitary
conditions were incredibly noisome. In most streets there were
open drains like broad ditches to carry away the sewage. In

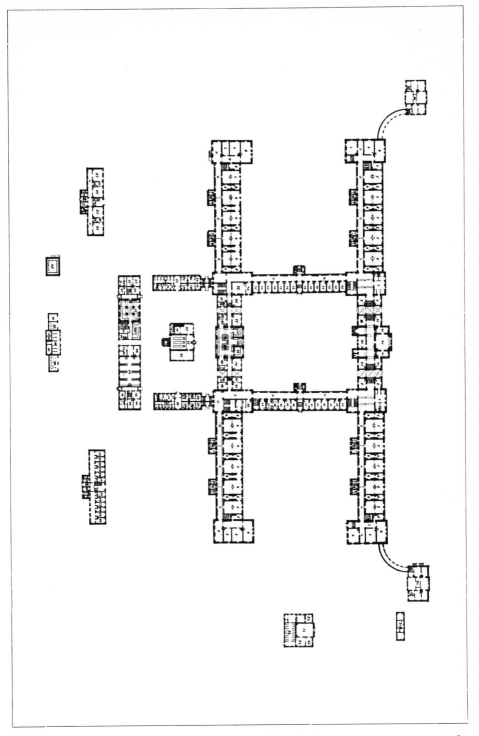

The City Hospital, Copenhagen. Ground floor plan in its original form. Scale 1 : 2000.

one of his fairy tales, *The Constant Tin Soldier,* Hans Andersen describes the debris that could be seen floating along the noxious stream—fascinating, undoubtedly, to small boys playing there but hardly healthy. A large percentage of the population lived in damp cellars. Drinking water was impure. Bath rooms and public baths were unknown.

There were very few people who realized how bad conditions were and no one had any idea how they might be improved. In the larger cities of other countries, where they were faced with the same problems, they had made some headway—at any rate, on paper. A young Danish doctor, Emil Hornemann, who had been on an extended study trip in England and France, roused sluggish consciences with disturbing articles about the inexcusable conditions rampant in the city. An Indian cholera epidemic had reached Europe and Copenhagen would be helpless if it were stricken by the plague.

Hornemann, in league with other sanitation specialists, fought for better conditions. They succeeded finally in getting a commission of health appointed but before its members could come to any conclusions the epidemic had reached the city (1853).

In the crisis the doctors proved that they could do more than stir up feeling. They worked heroically ministering to the sick. But they did something even more important. Hornemann and his co-workers organized the evacuation of the most crowded districts to improvised tent cities outside the walls. Without warning the congested city found itself spread out over unbuilt land. Thousands were finally living in tents and a careful statistical study proved that the spreading of the population was the best means of avoiding the danger.

The advantages of a low percentage of utilization of land, which earlier had been a pet theory of the hygienists, had now been proved in practice. When the epidemic was over these men devoted all their energy to the establishment of a colony of low dwelling houses which would relieve the congestion of the overcrowded flats in the oldest part of town.

M. G. Bindesbøll, the leading architect of the country who had built in Etruscan style the polychrome museum which houses Thorvaldsen's sculpture, entered enthusiastically into this less monumental project. He planned the new dwelling

Houses built by the Medical Association, looking down a cross-street between two parallel blocks. Sketched in 1948.

section as a self-contained little unit of two-storeyed brick buildings. Since then, the colony has grown twice as large with its own lecture hall, co-operative stores, laundry, and kindergarten. Originally it was surrounded by open fields; now its environment is completely urban but it still preserves its special character. It lies between two radial thoroughfares, fenced off from the streets and closed to through traffic. Its precincts are seldom disturbed by a motor vehicle.

Thus, while the great expansion of Vienna was inaugurated with the construction of imposing tenement blocks in the Ring district, Copenhagen was given the Medical Society's housing scheme as the best object lesson in the town-planning rule that "nothing is gained by overcrowding". In both cities constricting fortifications had for so long a time accustomed the populations to live in congested dwelling quarters that they had the impression that multi-storey houses were inevitable in a large city. This impression was not dispelled when the Copenhagen doctors demonstrated that there were other and better forms of dwellings. Despite the fact that they had so recently experienced all the horrors of a cholera epidemic, Copenhageners would rather try to imitate the grandeur of imperial Vienna than listen to the good advice of their medical practitioners.

In the 'fifties everyone knew that it was only a question of time before the walls of Copenhagen must fall and at some

153

distance beyond them, on the other side of the so-called demar-
cation-line, a flurry of uncontrolled building had taken place.
But inside the line building was still prohibited, which left a
broad, open area between the city and the new building district,
just as in Vienna. The first plan for the utilization of this area
was an ideal project prepared by a private architect in 1857,
the year in which the public competition took place in Vienna.
This Danish project gives expression to the same ideals as the
Vienna programme: broad boulevards lined with regular
blocks of dwellings interrupted only by squares containing
monumental buildings, arranged along symmetrical axes. The
entire area of the old fortifications with its broad moats and
tree-planted walls, which for so many years had formed a
delightful park belt around the city, was doomed by this plan
to be utterly destroyed.

The same year Hornemann wrote an article suggesting that
building should take place much farther out, where there was
cheap land to be had, so that workers' dwellings could be
assured plenty of light and air. There was no reason why
workers should not live some distance from the town. They
could travel back and forth by train — — "one day it will
have to come", he wrote. And he suggested the adoption of
cheap fares for workers, such as was later introduced in England by the Cheap Trains Act (1864).

No one lent a willing ear to these really modern ideas which
were regarded as completely Utopian. The State was interested
in filling its coffers by selling the hitherto unbuilt areas for
building purposes. The authorities were willing to raise the
ancient building bans in exchange for the payment of an as-
sessment by the land owners amounting to 50 % of appreciation on land values. Thus, both State and landlord were
equally interested in the exploitation of the area. A State Commission of engineers and artists—among them Christian Hansen—proposed a building plan which entirely ignored the
viewpoint of the hygienists. It was based on the assumption
that the land should be just as intensively utilized in the new
sections as in the old, for they actually feared that otherwise
the city might spread out over too great an area. They worked
on a population density of 300 per acre (750 per ha), corresponding to the density today in the most crowded quarters.

Copenhagen, the State Commission's plan of 1865. Scale 1 : 20.000.

There existed an unshakeable belief that when sanitation was in order, i. e. drinking-water and sewage, and broad paved streets and some few boulevards laid out, everything was as perfect as man could make it.

But this plan was not permitted to go unchallenged. Christian Hansen's ambitious colleague, architect Meldahl, who was also a member of the Academy of Art, published *his* plan, which proposed the preservation of the entire fortification terrain as a green belt and the construction of a monumental residential section beyond it between broad boulevards. This plan won many adherents but the one finally adopted was, nevertheless, a compromise. The government would not hand over the land to the municipal authorities without compensation and the city could not afford to pay the large sum demanded simply to procure a green belt. So it ended with the conversion of a part of the area into parks and a part sold as building land—poor land, at that, as for centuries it had been the city's fortification moats and was now badly filled in. The private landlords kept their property and were able to utilize it as intensively as they wished as long as they paid 50 % of appreciation to the city. The architect Meldahl succeeded in having a provision inserted in the building by-laws whereby it was permissible to add four feet to the normal building height for decorative cornices. The provision was extensively utilized; all buildings were provided with crowning cornices to make them as high as possible. As in Vienna, there was a great deal of ornament on the façades. Houses with grandiose fronts and domes and many towers were built facing the artificial lakes that had girded the city for centuries. Behind all this trumpery ornament (cheap at the time but now very expensive to keep up) lie some of Copenhagen's poorest and

Buildings along Søtorvet (Lake Square) Copenhagen.

Søtorvet, Copenhagen. Sketched in 1948.

Meldahl's Plan of January, 1866. Scale 1 : 20.000. North upward.

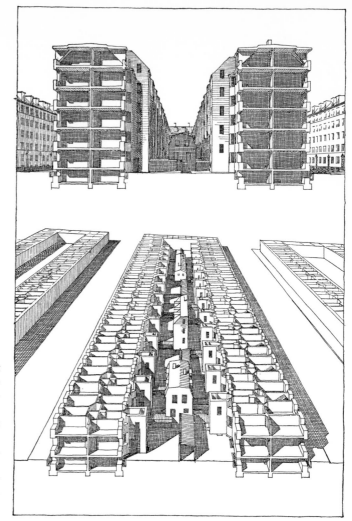

Typical example of building in the banlieues after the demolition of the walls. Two-room flats with kitchen stairways projecting into the court yards as staircase towers. Section in scale: 1 : 500. The courtyards are not very much broader than the central hall of Louis XIV's "small" Marly palace. (See p. 75).

most exploited dwelling sections with tiny flats and dark, narrow courtyards.

The course followed in the planning of the fortification areas from the moment that the demolition of the walls began to be discussed is nothing less than tragic. There were great opportunities to be grasped but they were all wasted. A hundred years ago there were already hygienic experts who realized how fatal the crowding of flats in tenement blocks was and who expressed their views in print and speech. There were also good architects, like Christian Hansen. The State and the city owned much land and still nothing better was produced than ornamental façades masking dark and dismal flats. The

over-crowding, which had been forced on a city hemmed in
by fortification walls, had now become the norm, elevated to
the dignity of a law for the new sections. Practically everyone
believed it must be so. Was not Copenhagen on its way to
become a metropolis? And in Berlin, Paris and Vienna it was
still worse.

What an architect like Christian Hansen could do when
he was able to follow his own convictions he had demonstrated
by building the city hospital which still stands as a model of *See plan page 151.*
what a hospital should be. It consists of a number of buildings
containing side corridors, linked together in the most natural
manner. It is a symmetrical structure, to be sure, but this is
quite inevitable in a building with a men's side and a women's
side. However, the symmetry is not carried to extremes. All
wards lie on the sunny side while on the other side are small
out-buildings containing lavatories and rooms with special in-
stallations. The simple rhythm of the façades, alternating with
two large and one small window, indicates clearly the size of
the rooms behind. All common rooms are centrally located:
In the middle, directly under the dome, is the hospital's chapel,
below it the operating room and administration offices. Further
back, but just as easy of access for the wards, are the hospital
kitchens, bath buildings and laundries. The hospital is well-
placed in relation to the "Ring" street with its long main wing
drawn somewhat back from the noise of traffic, with a small
doctor's house at each end.

While the dwelling houses of the day sought to compete
with the palaces of an earlier period by a lavish use of ornamental detail, the hospital is almost prosaic in its simplicity.
In Vienna Theophilus Hansen's imposing parliament building
was a fitting monument for the wealthy capital of a great empire. But no less fitting is the sober edifice Christian Hansen
created for the modest capital of a tiny kingdom—while in the
consistency of its design and execution it can well be compared
with the great monuments of former times.

Sketch from Palais Royal, a large enclosed garden in the center of Paris.

PARIS BOULEVARDS

There was a time when the Place des Vosges (originally the Place Royale) was the meeting-place of all Paris. Here the great tournaments took place; here friends strolled together under the arcades. But it was not long before Henri IV's square went out of fashion. The city drew westward (as most cities, strangely enough, do). There where Cardinal Richelieu had built his palace, Palais Cardinal, a great building enterprise was carried out in the 18th century. A four-winged block of uniform houses was erected around the old rectangular garden and given the impressive name of Palais Royal. At the ground-storey level arcades ran all the way round the building. It was not possible to drive into the square: from the adjoining streets one had to walk through the arcades to get there. It became a popular haunt, a gathering place for the idlers of the town who sauntered along the tree-shaded walks and hovered about the arcades. It soon was known as a place of very evil repute. Even before the Revolution the Palais Royal had been a resort of prostitution and gambling. During that great upheaval it became a news centre, a street forum. An English visitor wrote home: "All day long there were enormous multitudes of people in the Palais Royal. They stood so tightly packed that an apple that had been dropped from the balcony down on that pavement of heads never reached the ground." About the bookshops in the arcades he wrote: "The turmoil is beyond description. Every hour a new pamphlet appears."

The mob rule of the Revolution emanated from the Palais Royal. After Napoleon's fall it still played an important rôle in the life of the city. The heroes of Balzac's novels, which portray the reign of the "bourgeois king", Louis-Philippe, seek the gaming tables there to try to win back the fortunes they have squandered away.

But more and more this closed, tree-shaded square was abandoned for the open boulevards. Earlier, these had marked the outer boundaries of the capital but now they were surrounded by new districts on all sides. They were unrivalled for promenading and along the boulevards cafés and places of amusement flourished. Pictures of the period depict gay, friendly scenes with a rather small-town atmosphere. The new monarchy created few new thoroughfares but it did change the physiognomy of the old boulevards. Paris became a city of bourgeois amusements and real estate speculation. A list of the theatres, cafés, dance halls, and other attractions of the Paris of that day, is startling, to say the least. It conjures up visions, not of simple bourgeois pleasures but rather of hectic cosmopolitan life. The reader of Balzac's novels is fascinated by the vortex whirling through their pages, aghast at the life he describes. He shows us the reverse of the medal, the bourgeois monarchy corroded by money sharks and picaroons, by wanton prodigality and depraved poverty. It was a life that could but shock and offend those it did not enrich. The farther the Napoleonic era receded into the background, the more heroic and glorious it seemed to the French people. Forgetting the suffering it had caused, they romanticized the Empire. Louis-Philippe attempted to propitiate public opinion by completing the Arc de Triomphe, by bringing Napoleon's remains to Paris, and by other undertakings of the kind. But all this served only to place the king more and more in the shadow of the great emperor. The more he did to satisfy his people's unhealthy desire to romanticize and glorify the Napoleonic epoch, the easier he made it for those who were working for a new emperor. The man who was to assume this

The Paris boulevardier of the Louis Philippe era with his corsetted waistline and elegant, voluminous mantle with crimson silk lining. Note the "Turkish" restaurant in the background.

rôle was at first regarded as quite harmless. He had already attempted some coups d'états almost operetta-like in their dilettantism. He had written books in prison which were proof more of political pretentions than of statesman-like intelligence. And still he came more and more to the fore, riding on an emotional wave which he and his henchmen exploited and strengthened by clever propaganda, until at last Louis Napoleon was firmly established as president of the new Republic and well on his way to become the new emperor.

Once having attained power, the important thing was to consolidate his position. Ever since the Fronde revolt, during Louis XIV's minority, Paris had witnessed many street battles. During the fighting in 1848 a garrison had been cut off by the barricades erected in the narrow, crooked streets where artillery could not be brought into play. Long, broad, straight thoroughfares, in which the line of fire was not obstructed, was the best means of keeping down revolt. And the new Napoleon, who had come to power through revolution, knew how important it was to provide protection against assault from within. He stabilized his government so that it could not be overthrown except by military disaster. When he became president he immediately started planning a new Paris with straight building lines and broad thoroughfares which were not adaptable to the usual street-fighting tactics. The first work to be carried out was a continuation of his great ancestor's Rue de Rivoli and the beginning of a new, broad avenue at right angles to it: Boulevard de Strasbourg.

Napoleon's plans were presented to the inhabitants as a proposal for the beautifying of Paris and he saw to it that they became popular among the common people. But the upper classes were not very enthusiastic. The important thing, therefore, was to find a man big enough to take the responsibility and then to raise the enormous sums that would be necessary.

The man was found in 1853. His name was Georges-Eugène Haussmann, a Frenchman of German extraction. He had been chosen by one of Napoleon's supporters, the Minister of the Interior, Persigny, who describes him thus: "Big, fat, strong, energetic, and at the same time wily, always able to extract himself from difficulties, this daring man was not afraid to reveal his true character. As he sat there before me, explaining himself with brutal cynicism, I was not able to hide my lively satisfaction. I said to myself, *here* is the man we want. He will not be bothered by scruples about the means to be employed in the fight against the ideas and prejudices of a whole economic school, against people who are subtle and sceptical, people from the stock exchange and judicial circles. There, where the most distinguished, the most modest and unwavering nobleman must of necessity fail, there, this giant with his backbone of iron and his bull neck, full of audacity and cunning, prepared to deceive the deceiver and trap the trapper, will be sure of success. I enjoyed in prospect the thought of turning this brute loose among the snarling foxes and wolves ready to tear apart the noblest endeavours of the Emperor."

Georges-Eugène Haussmann in dress uniform. As Seine Prefect he was not only the chief administrator of Paris but he also had a seat in the government with the Emperor his only superior.

Haussmann became a true servant of Napoleon III. They understood each other. He was appointed Prefect of the Seine, the chief administrative officer of Paris. Before the appointment, the Emperor had — to satisfy the sceptical — delegated a commission of experts to take care of town-planning affairs. After the first meeting of the commission at which Haussmann was present, the Emperor detained him to hear what he thought of it. "Sire", he said, "I think the commission is much too large. The most trivial remarks easily become whole speeches and instead of short reports we are given learned treatises. The work would proceed more smoothly if the commission were presided over by the Emperor with the Seine Prefect as secretary whose duty it was to bring all questions before the commission and see that they were carried out. Between the Sovereign and his obedient servant there should be as few members as possible." "In other words", said the emperor, laughing, "preferably there should be none at all?" "Yes, that's just what I mean", replied Haussmann. "I believe you are right", said the emperor.

It was Haussmann, himself, who recapitulated this conversation in his memoirs, and he added: "I heard no more of the commission."

See: Mémoires du Baron Haussmann. 2. édition. II. page 57.

Now the path was clear for the Emperor's henchman.

Sweeping plans were ready for his genius. All over the city new thoroughfares were to be laid out in the form of boulevards, thirty meters wide, or more. Paris had been originally

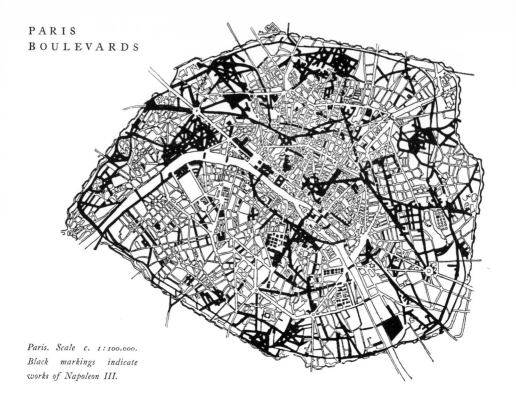

*Paris. Scale c. 1:100.000.
Black markings indicate
works of Napoleon III.*

built up by the Romans around a Seine crossing, a great inter-
section between roadway and waterway. But in the medieval
street network of the city the original plan was no longer visible. Through this intricate web of streets Napoleon III now
cut a broad artery straight across the island and over the river:
Boulevard de Strasbourg, Boulevard de Sebastopol, Boulevard
St. Michel: in all, four kilometers long. Corresponding to the
historic boulevards on the right bank, which once had been
city boundaries, the great Boulevard St. Germain was broken
through on the left bank. Corresponding to the old boulevard
which led in toward the Madeleine, came a symmetrical boulevard toward the northwest. Corresponding to the Place de
l'Etoile toward the northwest a similar *place* was laid out
toward the southeast. Even the outer districts were pierced
by long, straight boulevards.

164

The most impressive thing about Napoleon III's boulevards
is that they were actually carried out. It is a feat of energy
comparable to that displayed by a country at war when its
entire strength is concentrated on one aim: to support the
fighting forces. It is an example of what an absolute ruler can
accomplish who shuns no expedient — — in this case the
absolute ruler as a town-planner on the grand scale: quick,
visible results which would impress the world; plans made by
the emperor, himself, without previous study, based on his
infallibility, alone. It has been estimated that, in the 17 years
before Napoleon's fall, the enormous public works carried out
in Paris cost two and a half milliard francs. The state grants
for the work by no means amounted to this sum. The state
expropriated the land but, beforehand, private building contractors had agreed to demolish the old houses, erect new,
construct the boulevards and hand them over when finished
to the state which, then, over a period of years was to pay for
the work. To get the expropriation money, it was arranged
that the contractors, before taking over the work, were to lend
the necessary sums to the state.

All this was possible only because the Seine Prefect occupied
a unique position. He was not a minister but nevertheless he
had a seat in the cabinet and was responsible only to the
emperor who, in these matters, assumed absolute control.
Haussmann found the more or less correct means to carry out
the emperor's plans and the emperor protected and supported
Haussmann.

From a rational point of view Napoleon's whole scheme was
of very amateurish character when not directly based on older
plans. It is exactly what might be expected when town planning
is done by laying a ruler on a city map and, with no regard
for the cost, cutting great swaths straight through blocks of
houses.

To procure the land, alone, on which the great opera-
house was to be built, cost at the time not less than 30 million
francs, equal to about five million pounds today, and even at
that the site was far from ideal. The boulevards and avenues
are broad enough and the lively street scene they present is
interesting to the casual onlooker as he watches the difficulties of traffic at the many unreasonably sharp corners. But

165

*Napoleon III built his Paris
on the foundation of the
Paris of the monarchy. This
view from the time of the
Second Empire shows how
the great palaces had developed. In the foreground the
Tuileries (compare p. 57), to
the right the Louvre Gallery
connecting it with the Louvre.
To the left rue de Rivoli. In
the right hand background
Pont Neuf with the Place
Dauphine (compare p. 61)
and Notre Dame.*

it is not good in a technical sense. Napoleon III's town-planning consists of fire-belts drawn through a great city's jungle
but is remains a jungle despite them. Theis great undertaking
was meant to be both a slum clearance and a traffic reform;
it was to give work to the unemployed so that all could have
enough to eat, all feel proud and satisfied because of the great
things that were happening in Paris. Paid applause eulogized
the great social achievements all the while the gigantic works
were being pushed through by the most unscrupulous means

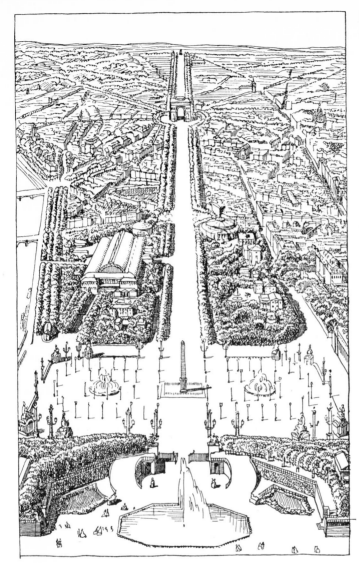

Champs Elysées, the great axis which, since the days of Louis XIV, had developed westward from the Tuileries Gardens. In the foreground the Garden followed by the Place de la Concorde originally laid out in honour of Louis XV - now his esquestrian statue has been replaced by an obelisk. From here the magnificent avenue leads up to the great Arc de Triomphe on the circular Place de l'Étoile from which twelve avenues radiate.

—— lining the pockets of cynical speculators. And it was the people who had to pay for it all and move from their small flats in the old houses to smaller and dearer ones in new houses that were higher than ever before, with windows opening on dark courtyards hidden from sight behind the fine stucco-façades lining the boulevards. The enormous levies of man-power and money helped not at all. They were both employed in the wrong places. The city was too concentrated. The correct solution would have been

167

to spread it out over a larger area. Napoleon and Haussmann had tried to accomplish this, but here they had no success. Neither did they succeed in utilizing the new means of mass transportation, the steam locomotive, to facilitate such spreading out. They feared bringing the railway into the centre of town and felt it should be used only for passage from one city to another. They did not, or *would* not, admit its importance for local traffic. In the 18th century the old fiscal walls, now demolished, had cramped the city within an iron ring. But it was really not much better off later with the railway forced to remain outside. The ideals admired by Napoleon were entirely reactionary. In the Rome of Pope Sixtus V (see p. 48) where only a very small area of the city within the walls was inhabited, it had been an excellent idea to draw long thoroughfares through the city so that pilgrims, on foot, could find their way from one great church to the other. But in 19th century Paris it was a little late to give chief consideration to earlier forms of locomotion. It became a city where the upper classes could take the air in their elegant horse-drawn vehicles but traffic was *not* employed to make possible better living conditions. Slum-clearance was carried out by tearing down immense numbers of houses (altogether about 3/7 of all houses in the city) and then laying out broad avenues and erecting new houses which, in a smaller area, were to contain as many, or more, flats. Furthermore, some of the space was utilized for cafés, restaurants and shops, designed first and foremost for tourists. Rents in the new buildings were high because they had to cover the interest on the land and on the house that had been torn down as well as on the new one erected in its stead. And the sum total of all this was more room for traffic but not more dwelling space for the people.

The architecture at the end of the century was not up to the standard of the time of Napoleon I and much inferior to that of the 18th century. But it was hidden by trees. The whole of Paris was to be a park system in which green avenues of trees united the individual small and large gardens or parks. Not many gardens remained from earlier times and these became even fewer after Haussmann had turned Paris topsy-turvy. In 1922 the then 78-year-old Anatole France wrote about the Paris he had known in his childhood,

During the reign of Napoleon III new boulevards were created for pleasure driving between rows of tall trees which had been transplanted at great cost.

before the time of Napoleon III: "Paris was friendlier then than it is today. The houses were lower, gardens more plentiful. Everywhere one saw rural tree tops extending over the old walls. The houses, which were all very different, stood forth individually, each with the special bouquet of its age and condition. Some of them, that once had been beautiful, preserved a melancholy dignity." Under Napoleon III the low houses and the trees with their rural tops disappeared. Instead, city trees were planted in long rows along the kerbs of the new broad boulevards. But if the trees in the streets resembled rigid rows of soldiers, the public pleasure grounds, on the other hand, were exceedingly romantic. Napoleon III's landscape gardener, Alphand, remodelled the two great woods, Bois de Boulogne and Bois de Vincennes, just outside Paris, in the so-called "English" style of the period, with rambling walks and lakes with irregular contours. When we see, in old illustrations, how beautiful they had been before, and when we recall past achievements of landscape gardening in France, we realize how mediocre Alphand's work was. It was dilettantism given the stamp of authority; the most childish ideas carefully drawn up and carried out by whole armies of workers.

Typical of the period is a park in northeast Paris. It is in a drab suburban district where even the boulevards are dismal and gloomy. There is no traffic to justify their great width.

This vignette does not picture a youth delivering a petition to Napoleon III from the victims of his amateurish town planning in Paris. It shows the Prince Imperial, himself, presenting his father with a medal for the Emperor's models for workers' homes exhibited at the World Exhibition of 1867. The Emperor had introduced the awarding of prizes for meritorious work and himself presented the main awards. Now that he was to receive the highest award for his achievement, his little son — the chairman of the Exhibition — was chosen to present it to him before a gathering of 18.000 people on July 1, 1867.

*The Parc des Buttes Chaumont
with its temple-crowned hill
rising precipitously from the
lake. After a romantic view
from the time of Napoleon III.*

*The Parc des Buttes Chaumont
sketched in 1937. Note the
lush vegetation of the hill
compared with the earlier
illustration above. The large
willow tree at left somewhat
reduces the size of the artificial promontory.*

The trees, too, are singularly grey. On the benches under them people loll and play checkers and unkempt children romp around them. Here, Napoleon III laid out a park almost as fanciful as the imperial gardens in Peking. Earlier it had been a rather desolate and disorderly place where great limepits formed a huge depression in the terrain. It had also been a place of execution. Now it became a park containing a lake from which rose a steep rocky island enhanced with artificial crags grottoes, cascades and a stone staircase winding upward, beneath overhanging trees to a round temple crowning the summit from where there is a sweeping view over Paris. A cable ferry connects the island "butte" with the shore, as does also a slender suspension bridge and another built to resemble a classic ruin. But this "Parc des Buttes Chaumont" is an important breathing-hole for the stuffy, grey suburb and hundreds of children use it for their playground. A little donkey cart drives round the winding paths and for a copper or two the children can have a romantic tour. They crowd round the refreshment booths where drops and lemonade are sold and mothers sit with their prams down by the lake ...

Paris continued to be a jungle —— and may not this very fact account for the great popularity it has always enjoyed? In the congested districts the people spent as much time in the streets as in-doors. Until late in the morning they stood half-dressed and sleepy-eyed hanging over the wrought iron bars outside the French windows. The shops displayed their wares

170

outdoors and even the smallest restaurants had sidewalk cafés where guests could sit watching the street scene. Here and there outdoor cafés with their colourful awnings seemed to line the whole length of the street. The centres of some of the boulevards were gay with vegetable markets where thrifty French housewives haggled over the wares. A man would come wandering through the street with several large, brown goats which he milked when customers stopped him. This was the city's supply of guaranteed fresh milk. People were goodnatured, gregarious and loquacious. There were not many children nor were conditions favourable for children, but those there were, were loved and admired. This Paris, where all cafés and restaurants were open from early morning to late night was a boon for visitors to the gay city.

Viewed from an aeroplane or a tower, Paris is a swarm of very tall houses interspersed with gloomy wells of courtyards and with broad boulevards radiating from large *ronds points*. A typical bird's-eye-view of a *London* residential section gives quite another picture: endless rows of two- or three-storey attached houses, behind them narrow garden plots, in the streets and gardens many children.

As in the foregoing centuries, nineteenth century London developed entirely differently than Paris. In London there was no dictatorial command from above to break new roads through the old street network. But private initiative worked steadily to spread out the town and give it means of transportation between the ever further outlying communities and London City, which became a purely business district. The first railway, 1834, was a suburban line from London to Greenwich. It was followed by a veritable railway mania. In 1845 there were no less than 19 proposals for London lines. As early as 1854 permission was granted for the first underground railway. This proved to be an effective instrument for the decentralization of the city.

Thus, Paris and London continued to go their separate ways, Paris still the congested city with boulevards like enormous monuments commemorating an absolute government, London more and more the decentralized city with the Underground to bring people to the outlying districts — — — in its way just as great an achievement as the Paris boulevards.

Paris restaurant. It is located in one of the old buildings in the Place Dauphine from the time of Henri IV. (Compare pp. 56 & 60.) The restaurant is tiny but in its almost microscopic kitchen a long list of delectable dishes are conjured forth. There is a sidewalk café out toward the Seine as well as in the quiet old square, now lined with spreading trees. The few outdoor tables are occupied at all hours by a constantly changing stream of guests of all qualities and kinds. At one of the tables there may be several artisans who work in the neighbourhood, at another American tourists, at a third French artists in colourful smocks and velvet trousers, and at a fourth a couple of Danes who quickly feel at home in the friendly, democratic atmosphere which lends added zest to the delicious food.

171

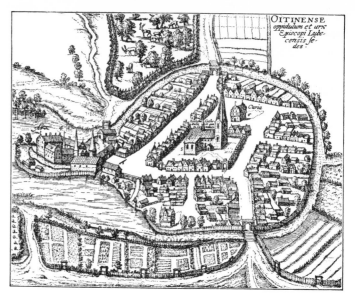

LAND AND SPECULATION

Since the Middle Ages city forms have undergone many
changes. Briefly, it may be said that the shape of medieval
towns was usually determined by the ring of fortifications,
the protective city walls, and this was also more or less true
of Renaissance cities. But during the reign of Absolutism the
form of the city was influenced by the demand for a visible,
representative unity symbolizing the new centralized authority.
In the 19th century, on the other hand, it was the *modus
operandi* of land speculation which left its impress on most
cities. The main object of the enormous housing schemes of
the period was not to provide security or to embellish the city,
nor was it to produce decent living accommodation for the
tenants; its sole object was to provide large and safe incomes
for the promoters. In our century we have been trying in
various ways to extricate ourselves from the web of speculation
so that we can make cities pleasant and healthy to live in.

In the Middle Ages it was natural to take land for granted.
It was there, and there was more than enough of it. Its value
depended on whether or not it was arable, and when it ceased
to be cultivated it became worthless again. Therefore, the
ground on which buildings stood had no value in itself and,
consequently, could not be made an object of speculation. The
buildings, alone, could be bought and sold.

The Church was the first to realize that city land could be made to pay. The churches owned large areas of urban property which acquired special value as holy places to which people made pilgrimages from all over the country. Lucrative returns could be obtained by parcelling out the church domains into very small plots and selling them for the erection of booths from which candles, holy pictures, and even quite mundane articles might be sold. Soon a group of small buildings encircled the base of the church and the teeming life around them served to emphasize the solemn majesty of the sacred edifice.

Otherwise urban property was not sold. Since early in the Middle Ages, however, cities — which owned land as a matter of course — had received rent incomes from houses and land. At first the tenant was given a one-year lease with the implicit right to renew it from year to year. Little by little this developed in the towns, just as in the country, into tenancy for life or for a term of years, still at a yearly rental. Something of the same sort still exists today in England, where land is let on long leases both in town and country. The landlord is assured a steady income and full dominion over his property. The owner may be a city, a university, a guild, a church, an estate, or some other perpetual institution not dependent on the life and death of an individual.

Absolutism was not interested in conditions which made possible a great accumulation of power alongside that of the State, and, therefore, medieval tenancies were gradually terminated in continental cities. Towns, universities and schools lost their incomes from urban property and became, as a consequence, more dependent on the State.

The development in Copenhagen is typical. At one time long-term tenancies had also been the rule there. But as early as the 16th century fixed tenancies were brought to an end. Instead of the old, clear contract whereby those who used the property were tenants with definitely limited rights, new, vague conditions made them landlords of a sort, with the right to sell the land and, on the whole, to do with it as they pleased, so long as they paid the annual rent. Both parties concerned, the original owner and the new proprietor, were quite satisfied with the arrangement. The former continued to receive the payment of yearly rent and had not the slightest obligation in

return; the latter obtained what *he* wanted, the unconditional
use of the property and the right to sell it if he so desired. For
them both the transaction meant the least amount of friction
and the greatest freedom of action. But here arose a fatal mis-
understanding — it was taken for granted that the rental sum
was fixed once and for all. And there was one thing which the
landlord did not take into consideration, which, indeed, nobody
did. That was the falling value of money, inflation. The yearly
rent, which originally had been a tangible asset, dwindled
little by little, as the purchasing power of money decreased,
until finally it was no more than a nominal sum, of small value
to its possessor. In 1688 Copenhagen was already complaining
of the inadequacy of incomes from rents. In England, where
long-term leasing of land — both urban and rural — had never
ceased, rents were raised every time a lease expired. But in
Copenhagen no one even thought of the possibility of raising
rents. On the contrary, in 1725 the town council received royal
authority to negotiate with tenants for an acquittal sum once
and for all. The Copenhagen of today might have been a
wealthy city if, instead of abolishing rents, the city fathers of
the 18th century had arranged for them to rise simultaneously
with appreciation of real estate values. The medieval church,
too, had, as already mentioned, been a great landlord. But
during the Reformation the churches had lost most of their
property. Much church real estate had been transferred to
private individuals at no other cost to them than the payment
of annual rents. Thus, both city and church gradually lost
possession of their landed property. But at the time no one
was aware of what was really happening, because the process
took several centuries.

It is quite understandable that the farther the domestic
economy of the Middle Ages receded into the past, the less
the possession of real property interested the civic authorities.
In Feudal times municipal officers were generally given rent-
free dwellings for their labours as well as the right to cultivate
city-owned land. Now they were being paid with money, and
the money was procured by means of taxation. City-owned land
was no longer necessary. Neither was it necessary for the city
itself to own property in order to enforce such building re-
strictions as were deemed advisable for the good of the com-

munity. This could be arranged by passing building laws and
ordinances. It all seemed so easy but it proved to be very difficult. The tradesman who thinks in terms of concrete goods,
goods with which he is thoroughly familiar, does not so easily
find himself in dangerous situations as does the speculator who
deals with *paper* values, the intrinsic nature of which he does
not understand. Cities soon found themselves in the situation
of the speculator.

Never before had cities been faced with such great problems
as in the 19th century. But no one was really aware of them.
On the contrary, everyone heaved a sigh of relief. The iron
hold which guild and crown had had on the towns was broken.
The privileges of the aristocracy had been reduced. The era
of the new industrialists and bankers had dawned. There was
great rejoicing over the tremendous technical progress which
everyone believed would bring happiness and prosperity to
mankind. Merchandise, which earlier had been produced slowly
and painstakingly by hand, could now be made by machine,
and machines could be operated by cheap labour. A vast flood
of workers poured into urban centres creating a demand for
cheap dwellings on an hitherto unheard of scale.

Even workers' families which subsisted on starvation wages,
must have roofs over their heads. They obtained only the most
primitive lodgings and had to pay too much even for them.
House-owning became a lucrative business. But no one concerned with land speculation or house building felt any sense
of wrong-doing. If anyone hinted at the disgraceful living conditions of the poor, Society's answer concurred with the words
of the German, Treitschke, who, in a pamphlet on Socialism
and its supporter (1873), wrote: "Every human being is
first and foremost responsible for his own acts; and no one is
so badly off that he cannot hear God's voice in his sanctum".
It was the natural order of things — that is to say, the Will
of God — that some were rich and some poor. It was hopeless
to attempt to interfere with economic laws as the absolute
rulers had done. You could try to alleviate the conditions of
the poor by deeds of Christian charity, by giving alms to the
deserving, whose lot it was to live on the seamy side of life.
But, on the whole, it was perfectly clear that Divine Provid-
ence would insure progress better than all the palladiums of

the old regime. If man did not presumptuously interfere,
people would neither pay too much nor too little for the ne-
cessities of life; and, thanks to the marvelous technical development, there would be more than enough for all and everything
would be cheap. The relationship between supply and demand
would determine prices. When the demand became very great,
interest in the production of a commodity would grow, new
and improved methods would be employed, the supply increase
and prices fall.

But this theory did not apply to houses and the land on
which they were built. On the Continent there was certainly
no lack of demand for land on which to erect small workers'
dwellings and, as most towns had only recently grown beyond
the old city walls, there was also land enough to use. But this
did not give cheap land; on the contrary, real estate prices
rose so that cheap, small houses could not pay. Building lots
are a commodity which does not deteriorate or go out of fashion
or in other ways lose value by being held back from the market.
The enormous growth of urban populations gave all city land-
holders the hope of sharing in the booty simply by waiting for
the psychological moment to build. For of course the greatest
profit would be obtained by holding on to property until time
was ripe for the most intensive exploitation of the land. No
other commodity offered such possibilities. Every house built
on it would continue to pay interest far into the future. The
speculator in land, who had sowed nothing, who had produced
nothing, was assured a golden harvest for himself and his
descendents as a reward for having been farsighted enough
to wait.

The value of a piece of property was, in other words,
proportionate to the number of dwellings that could be
squeezed on to it. No one was so weak-minded as to under-
sell his competitors, for there could be no advantage in doing
so. If a land-owner could not afford to bide his time until the
building boom had reached the neighbourhood of his property,
he could always sell it to a colleague who *could* wait, or he
could take a loan on it. Real estate was good security and in
Prussia and Denmark well-established loan institutions made
it possible for even the smallest landlords to benefit from this
great land boom.

The typical development of a continental city was as follows: first, new streets were marked out on the outskirts
of the town. A sewage system was installed and sidewalk
curbstones and lamp-posts appeared. Usually, building began
on corner plots. Very quickly houses sprang up as high as the
local by-laws permitted. They stood alone, looming ghost-like
in the midst of bare fields, with great, blank party-walls facing
the weed-covered neighbouring plots, grim omens of what the
future had in store. The land had become polluted. Nothing
could save it any longer. It was condemned to be covered with
real estate speculation's bleak barracks, with paving stones and
courtyard concrete. Who, now, would bother to erect friendly
small cottages and lay out gardens in the shadow of high, blank
walls? The land might remain empty for ten or twenty years,
or even longer, but eventually they would come, those tall,
dreary tenements closely crowded together, inhabited by
thousands of pale, tired workers.

Earlier, slum districts arose in neighbourhoods where one-
family houses had fallen into decay and had been made over
into rent barracks in which each separate room often housed
an entire family. This was still the case in London. But on
the Continent the great land boom led to the standardization
of these degraded conditions by the erection of whole districts
of jerry-built tenement houses filled with flats in which there
was no direct daylight or ventilation or even such simple
ameliorations as access to a bit of garden or just a view of green
trees. At first, large and small flats were found in the same
quarter. The better flats had living-rooms facing the street
and bedrooms in wings looking on a court, while at the back,
facing a narrow courtyard, the cheaper flats were found in
rear buildings. This was the case in the Gammelholm section
of Copenhagen, which had been built up before the old city
walls disappeared. Classes were now divided up in "front
house residents" and "back house tenants", where earlier they
had been separated by storeys. But later on classes separated.
Entire districts of workers' dwellings arose while more
fashionable neighbourhoods contained buildings with larger,
expensive flats, but both categories were characterized by that
intensive exploitation of the land which had come to be
regarded, on the Continent, as normal for great cities.

Courtyard interior showing distance between rear buildings of a Copenhagen tenement block in the Gammelholm district. The "front" buildings have large flats while the rear buildings include only tiny ones. Behind each window is the home of a tenant whose only view is of a courtyard like the one pictured here.

177

*Courtyard dwellings, Gam-
melholm, Copenhagen.*

There was colossal strength in land speculation. It could crowd houses together beyond all reason and force them high into the air. Napoleon III and Haussmann harnessed it to their Paris plans. In Vienna it created vast districts of one-room flats along dark corridors in rear buildings, often with a second and even a third building behind it. Berlin was also provided with enormous working-class neighbourhoods with one-room flats as the normal type of dwelling.

In Copenhagen the two-room flat predominated. By building bylaws an attempt was made to put a stop to the worst types of dwelling. One-room flats in rows along narrow, dark corridors, of which there were forbidding examples in older parts of the town, were banned. To avoid the erection of those extremely undesirable rear houses, the depth of building plots was reduced by laying the streets of new districts closer together. New regulations were also made to assure sufficient daylight in new buildings. But the by-laws were still inad-eequate. The men who made the laws, like most others, were so convinced that closely built tenements were a natural phe-nomenon of large cities that it simply did not enter their minds to suggest legislation which would revolutionize build-ing. Above all, it was against the entire spirit of the age to interfere radically with the owner's right to dispose of his property as he wished, even when it was a question of public health. Indeed, the new by-laws served, rather, to further the building of tenement houses instead of hindering it. As all paragraphs pre-supposed the construction of multiple dwell-ings, the demands they made were reasonable enough for these but raised the construction costs of one-family houses con-siderably and made their erection difficult by an unwieldy and costly administration.

In other words, the free play of economic forces could not provide cheap land for low-rent dwellings. Nor could build-ing legislation help the humbler members of society. Land-owners and their backers formed an unofficial cartel with a monopoly that had the poor in search of homes completely in its power. Their only chance was to become landlords, themselves. And though they did not have much money, they were in the majority. By joining forces, by co-operation, they could become an economic factor of importance. This was realized in England where workers' building societies were formed to buy land and build houses for members. Later, workers in other countries followed suit.

In Copenhagen a change in the official view of the right of the municipality to participate in building did not occur until the last decades of the 19th century, when the city was finally permitted to purchase land and construct model workers' dwellings. At the end of the century a number of large farms, lying just beyond the old city limits, were purchased. This step was to have a decisive influence on future development. As the town spread out toward the open fields, the municipality was able to sell land relatively cheaply for idealistic enterprises. This forced down the price of privately owned land. At last a landlord had appeared who was interested in selling cheaply enough to drive a wedge into the old land monopoly.

*Row of houses in a Workers'
Building Society settlement,
Copenhagen.*

As land on the outskirts of a large city must often lie unused for a long time before it can earn any increment, municipal land purchases cannot be counted on to give quick returns. But this is of secondary importance. The primary object of such investments is to facilitate an ordered planning of the city's development, which is very difficult to accomplish when the municipality is not a landlord. But as land purchases do not always give a profit in the first instance, it is worth investigating whether it would not be best for the city to retain title, as was earlier done, so that, when the time is ripe, the community can reap the profit of its investments. It is impossible to revert entirely to the medieval practice of leasing land for building purposes when building is financed by loans from credit and mortgage associations. In other words, the municipality must find a way to share in profits through increase in land values without hindering the financing of building. In Copenhagen all these questions were put in the hands of a commission and in 1906, following the recommendations made in its report, the city adopted the practice of selling land with the right of repurchase after 80—90 years, or its reversion to the community. In later years Copenhagen has been selling land on conditions still more favourable to the city. Now, after a period of time long enough for all loans to have been amortized, the buildings, too, revert to the city without compensation to the owners. This corresponds roughly to the conditions of long-term leases in many parts of London. Thus, by 1951, Copenhagen had returned to the ownership terms of the Middle Ages.

It is not only in Copenhagen that the importance of public ownership and control of land has been recognized. A survey of town-planning will show that there have been well-planned cities since the earliest times but only in places where all the land was in one hand, whether a state, a town or a private landlord. But from the moment in which the ownership of the land is shared by many small landlords with all their egoistic interests, total planning and control of development are almost impossible.

The 20th century has been endeavouring in many ways to improve the conditions handed down to it by the 19th century. Attempts are being made by communities to regain some of the authority they lost when they gave up land ownership by increasing their power through laws and administration which reduce the private owner's control of his property. The complex system of building by-laws found in most large cities can, naturally, grow so great that private ownership becomes illusory. But, to date, this method has not shown good results. It seems to lead to an excessive bureaucracy which interferes in every detail, large or small, and leaves decisions to the personal judgment of an office clerk. But it has not proved capable of creating anything new. Legislation hinders private planning at the same time that private boundaries hinder public planning. The easiest way out of this vicious circle is public ownership of the land. This makes possible permanent improvements and long-range planning, while security of tenure and as little interference as possible give the tenant all the freedom he needs.

Other communities are attempting to gain public control over the land, without actually owning it, by means of land taxes. If landlords were obliged to pay all profits made on their property in the form of a land tax, there would no longer be any incentive to land speculation with all its unfortunate results, and planning could be carried on without taking the economic interests of land-owners into consideration.

In those countries in which the question of better town-

planning is most acute, the problem of land speculation vs.
a large percentage of the population lives in towns, and where
the uncontrolled development of the great industrial cities has
created serious problems, this question has been studied by
several commissions. It is considered a matter of national importance. It is not a question of what is best for the individual
piece of property, or even the individual city, but for the entire
nation. Land speculation can lead to an unfortunate crowding
together of dwellings or factories, and it can be responsible
for a number of such drawbacks as poor hygienic conditions
or unreasonable transportation expenses. If a planning authority with a sufficient amount of power were to decide that
housing should be redistributed, moved to more favourable
localities and spread out more, some landlords would undoubtedly lose thereby, but the total value of the country's land
would not be reduced: indeed, it might even be increased if
the result of these housing improvements were a greater efficiency of labour in the country as a whole. In other words,
better planning can, theoretically, shift existing land values
but it cannot destroy them. But the practical problem for a
capitalistic society with private ownership of land is how to
make possible better planning, with its unavoidable limitation
of private rights, without expense to the community. Compensation claims will be forthcoming from those who lose by
it, but income to the community from those who gain will be
more difficult to secure.

In 1937 a commission was appointed in England, commonly
known as the "Barlow Commission", after its Chairman, Sir
Montague Barlow. Its work was to enquire into the causes
which have influenced the present geographical distribution
of the industrial population of Great Britain and the probable
direction of any change in that distribution in the future; to
consider what social, economic or strategical advantages arise
from the concentration of industries or of the industrial population in large towns or in particular areas of the country;
and to report what remedial measures if any should be taken
in the national interest.

It recommended the formation of a government body, The
National Industrial Board, with very far-reaching authority

to determine where future building might or might not
take place; suggesting, among other things, that the new
Board should immediately prohibit the establishment of new
industrial enterprise in London. Sir Patrick Abercrombie, a
member of the Commission, in an article accompanying the
report, wrote: "No real improvement in the control of land
development is possible until the fundamental question of
compensation and betterment is adequately resolved."

The Scott Committee, which was appointed in 1941, highly
recommended national planning in its report made in 1942.
Finally, the Uthwatt Committee's report of the same year
discussed the difficult economic problems of national planning.
The Committee decided against nationalisation of the land as
being not practicable as an immediate measure, and recommended the purchase by the State of development rights.

In the "Town and Country Planning Act", which was
passed by Parliament in 1947, this recommendation has been
followed. According to § 10 of this Act no new utilization
of land may take place after June 1948 without special permission. Examples are given of changes in use which do not
need special permission, and, as an example of one which does,
the installation of several flats in a house originally intended
for one family is named. For depreciation in the value of
property which was "ripe" for future development, compensation is to be paid from a fund of 300 million pounds. On
the other hand, every one who receives permission to utilize
his property in a new way which will increase its value shall
pay for the right to do so. In this way the Government hope
to recover the cost of the compensation to be paid.

And here the work of this whole problem ends for the
present. The vicious and unbridled speculation of the 19th
century must be abolished in the 20th century and the community must take over risks, responsibilities and technical
planning.

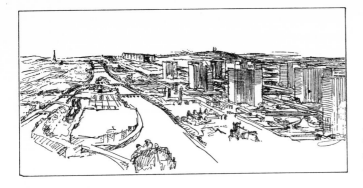

FUNCTIONALISM

Functionalism is often spoken of as a kind of moral conception, a belief that if things were made to fulfil a specific function, and with no other object in mind, a new sort of beauty would be the result. Others say that it is only a flash in the pan, a mode that is already practically passé. But far from being just another whim of fashion, it is, rather, the beginning of a new way of looking at things which, in time, will disclose its true importance. Functionalism is something very much more complicated than a banal moral principle.

This is not the first time that a change in man's entire conceptual framework has, little by little, permeated all fields of cultural activity. We have already seen how the discovery of perspective taught Europeans to see things in a new light. The painters led the way by giving people a feeling of depth, making it possible for them to sense the force of gravity. Sculptors were also architects, and they made their buildings like magnificent monuments, resting firmly on the ground and built up in broad layers of horizontal terraces, one over the other, to a magnificent whole. This was diametrically opposed to the building ideals of the preceding period.

The Gothic architect had admired the heavenward aspiring; his buildings seemed to *defy* the law of gravity. He was a master of elegant and daring construction and his masterpiece was the great cathedral. Inside were whole forests of very slender pillars rising to breath-taking heights where they bent toward each other like the branches of trees. The exterior was an immense framework of buttresses and arches which sustained the structure at just those points where its thin shell was

183

in danger of bursting apart. The Gothic cathedral was like a magnificently prepared skeleton from which all traces of muscle and skin had been removed. And this skeletal appearance was enhanced by the fact that all the buttresses tapered off into slim spires embroidered with lace-like tracery. Medieval masons had experienced naive pleasure in making these architectural miracles stand upright, and the myriads of details had filled them with joy. And then along came the Renaissance and found their work barbaric, found it "gothic", a style for half-civilized Goths, who — compared to the ancient Greeks and Romans — lacked the culture necessary to appreciate form for its own sake, independent of construction and all distracting details.

We have seen these two conceptions clash when, in 1665, the great sculptor and architect, Bernini, came from classical Rome to the Gothic Paris of the musketeers. The French capital, with its towers and spires and steep roofs, reminded him, he said with disdain, of the toothed instrument used for carding wool. While Gothic architects had taken great pride in making their edifices appear amazingly light and delicate, the aim of the masters of the new style was to make *their* buildings seem even heavier and more massive than they actually were. Impressive splendour had taken the place of daring and elegance.

Another illustration of the clash between the two conceptions can be seen in the expedition of the Spanish Armada against England in 1588, a trial of strength between the highly cultivated, formal Spain and the still quite Gothic, loosely-organized England. The Spanish ships magnificently represented a culture which repressed and hid the constructive and functional under ever-richer symbols and forms. They were like dazzling palaces that had broken away from their moorings and put to sea. They made their best showing when lying in the lee of the shore. There, life went on almost as on dry land. Life on board was a continuous pageant, subject to the rules of drama; a stylized life in which everyone had his rôle to play and the appropriate costume for it. This gave great assurance and dignity in all social intercourse but made for small efficiency in the work on hand. The Spanish form of naval warfare was as stereotyped as court ceremony. On board there were class distinctions not only between the noble officers and the enlisted men, but also between the ship's crew and the fighting troops. The object of these heavy, towering galleons was to bring the troops to the battle area. There were many more soldiers on board than seamen. The sailors' job was simply to bring the ships to the scene of battle and manoeuvre them into position. Then the soldiers took over and joined battle just as if they were on dry land. But the English were not so over-civilized nor so pompously organized. Their scraped-together fleet was a sorry sight compared to the Royal Armada, but their vessels were easy to manoeuvre. And the crews were very much more skilled in their handicraft, that of both soldier *and* sailor.

This struggle between pomp and circumstance on the one hand, and the unpretentious and efficient on the other, is the cause of a never-ending controversy. Absolutism employed the former to its own ends and, since Absolutism's fall, bourgeois society has never dared to give it up entirely. European civilization has retained a number of symbols of dignity as survivals of an earlier time.

When we see a picture of young men of the 'nineties, they look to us like grandfathers, so solemn and stiff with their beards, their starched shirts and collars, their dark and uncomfortable clothes. The stiff shirt-front, alone, was a marvel of discomfort, a completely useless article of dress, nothing more than a class symbol. It was easy to see that the wearer could perform no physical labour when he had it on. Compared to these *fin de siècle* beaux, the young men of today seem mere children in their plaid shirts and shorts. In summer we see them set off on their bikes, lightly clad, unconcerned with dignity, avid for adventure, fully and gloriously alive. Within one generation a revolution has taken place which we already take completely for granted.

The desire to attain great efficiency is not new. Industry and trade have always sought the most practical forms, the most labour-saving methods. The sober lettering of the typewriter has long since replaced the dash and swing of handwriting. But labour-saving was respectable only when employed in the business of making money. After working hours the last generation preferred to appear as men of leisure who could

Two typical young students of the 'nineties.

afford an inconvenient and ceremonial way of life — they abhorred "bohemians" who enjoyed life. One of the first motion picture strips ever taken, Lumière's film of lunch-hour at a factory in 1895, shows a group of young French working girls rushing out of a mill — poor, underpaid females, but every one of them clad in inappropriate clothes with hourglass waists and innumerable skirts that sweep the ground.

When young ladies played lawn tennis they were just as inappropriately dressed as their factory sisters. To begin with, the very idea, alone, of going outdoors to play games with young men, instead of remaining decorously indoors pursuing lady-like activities as their mothers and grandmothers had done, was in itself rather suspicious. But even though the fashion of the moment dictated outdoor sports and everyone believed they were important for health, it was certainly not necessary to give up all claim to decency for their sake. The ironclad female wardrobe was a last stand. When the game demanded that young ladies — in company with the opposite sex — do a thing so unlady-like as to run — at times even jump — it was important that their costumes observe the demands of respectability if the game were not to degenerate into out-and-out barbarism. Under no circumstances must the material be so light that a treacherous breath of wind might raise the skirt. The costume must combine great weight with voluminous width. To-day it is difficult for us to imagine what lawn tennis was like in the 'eighties and 'nineties. It is necessary to conjure up a vision of pale-faced young women with small hats perched on top of mounds of hair and held there firmly by veils drawn down under the chin and fastened at the nape of the neck: or, in the case of the more emanicipated, with mannish boaters held in place by hat-pins. The maidenly bosoms, encased in tight-fitting sheaths with enormous puff-sleeves, gently swayed hither and yon over the tennis courts, carried along by billowing yards of colourful materials... And the men, too, for that matter, were inappropriately clad in too many garments, and hats.

But in the long run this could not go on. The game had its idea, its rules, and they were essentially different from the rules of ordinary social intercourse, which had dictated the form of these clothes. A Victorian, approaching a tennis court with racquet in hand, must have felt he was entering a new world. He had, indeed, left his natural environment of plush and tassels and knick-knacks far behind; that world where nothing was allowed to appear in its naked form, where even a piano-leg was hidden under flounces and draperies. To enter the unadorned rectangle of the tennis court must have been like diving into bracing salt water in Spring, after a Winter spent by the fireside in woollens and velveteen. Was it not with something of a thrill the players approached those naked courts where everything was mathematically determined, with not the slightest decorative touch? Ah! that tennis game our Victorian ancestors played, with its timid little underhand serve — how far it was from the efficient game of to-day! Nevertheless, the tennis court was the one place where, for the pure fun of it, a technique was practised that had been inspired by rationalism. On five continents young people ardently studied the problem of how to send the ball over the net so that their opponents could not return it. Each new year brought more effective methods. No professional work was studied more thoroughly or carried out more conscientiously. These exploits, in which split seconds made all the difference, in which every muscle must be under control, necessitated thoroughly tested equipment, and could not be carried out in costumes designed for the needs of ordinary social life. Thus it was that the game of tennis helped to procure more and more comfortable clothes, until, to-day, tennis shorts for both sexes are universally accepted.

Through sport and its accompanying competition the upper classes learned to appreciate unadorned beauty. A new idea of style came into being. From the broken rhythm of the dances of an earlier day, with their bows and courtesies, the world moved on to the continuous, unbroken motion of sport, which shuns the superficial and concentrates on efficiency. Its intrinsic quality entered into the luxuries of the day, such as the pleasure yacht, the racing shell, and the stream-lined automobile. But people lived — and still live — simultaneously in two worlds which have nothing in common. At the end of the 19th century blocks of flats were considered particularly handsome when built in period styles. Thus, while architecture was seeking inspiration from the work of past centuries, the modern bicycle

FUNCTIONALISM was designed, a marvel of steel and rubber and thin wire spokes, which purred gently as it skimmed over the countryside. In the early days of silent motion pictures in Denmark, a film was being made which was set in the time of the Renaissance king, Christian IV, and his castle of Rosenborg in Copenhagen was used as a background for the suitably costumed actors. But, somehow or other, a bicycle, leaning against the castle wall, was overlooked and the entire film had to be taken over again. Such anachronism was unthinkable in a motion picture. But in real life it caused no comment. In real life people actually lived in a muddle of past and present: a *past* that saw beauty in the ornate and massive, and a *present* that was developing a taste for elegant, almost weightless things, devoid of ornament but absolutely not indifferent or accidental in form.

There *were* people who clearly saw the cultural discord of a period in which houses and furniture were made exactly like those of older periods, while other accessories of daily life were given entirely new forms. Instead of seeking *motifs* in historical buildings, the artist was advised to turn to nature, which was timeless. In Paris, French firms were in full swing producing beautiful things inspired by the cactus, the artichoke, the wood anemone, the pine cone, the water-lily, etc. In nature, particularly in plants and flowers, industrial art was to find renewal. This cultivation of nature at the end of the 19th century brought new blood not only to industrial art but also to architectural design, which was influenced by the lines of flowers. There was to be no more angular stiffness in architecture. Slim iron pillars, like gigantic flower stalks, shot up through the buildings, and from them vines branched out over the ceilings and the glass of skylights. It was a style in keeping with the tendencies in painting. Japanese woodcuts and drawings had created the greatest sensation in European art circles. Here was an art which ignored perspective and gravity. It was interested only in transposing nature studies into elegant, rhythmic lines and clear colours, without shadows.

Victor Horta: Wrought iron column from house in rue de Turin, Brussels. Erected 1893.

Artists began producing paintings and drawings that were very different from the historical pictures that had been the fashion for so many years; and architects saw new possibilities for an architecture that was rhythmic and light.

This new style, called "art nouveau", actually became popular, but like Gothic, Renaissance and Rococo, it was just another guise to add to the style masquerade. It was now possible to buy "art nouveau" furniture instead of Queen Anne or Jacobean, but the basic forms remained the same: panel sofas, sideboards fitted with shelves for displaying silver, "diplomat" writing tables, "what-nots", centre tables, stands for potted plants, china cabinets, screens, dressing tables, washstands. The ornamentation, alone, was different. The time had not yet come when furniture would be built that was just as beautiful *and* practical as, for example, the new sports equipment. Indeed, the more the new style gained ground, the further it led down a blind alley.

If a new architecture was to come into being it must be one that could solve modern problems better than traditional architecture had succeeded in doing. New ideals must be the basis of it — as they were of sport.

Between the two world wars a start had been made in this direction. People learned to appreciate other values than the brick foundation, the impressive façade, the representative interior. An out-of-doors movement started on a scale never seen before. During the summer months people left their good, solid homes to live in tents. They discovered how beneficial it could be to be released from the shackles of worldly goods and of class distinctions in dress and living customs. Ceremonious apparel, such as the frock-coat, stiff shirt, high wing collar and "Ascot" tie, became almost obsolete. Instead, the loose-fitting, comfortable attire of the sportsman became the ideal.

It was again the art of painting that came to the assistance of architecture and inspired it to new forms of expression. Just as, earlier, the pictorial arts had taught the European to see things in perspective, to perceive them as heavy, plastic bodies, modern painting now taught him to see beauty where there was no bulk. The painted surface, itself, in its play of colours, could possess artistic value entirely independent of all perspective and all illusion of space. The artist sought again the ideals of pure painting to take the place of the narrative and romantic art which had particularly interested the 19th century. The observer was not to ask himself what the picture represented but to notice the pattern formed by the interplay of colours

Henry von de Velde: Stand for a potted palm. The lower shelf was for a fern. — In all furniture the lines were to be as expressive as possible. — The elaborately curved legs of this stand, despite its extremely simple function, is typical of Art Nouveau.

189

Le Corbusier: Sketch for a one-family house. Roof-garden.

and lines. In other words, earlier, the planes of the picture had been regarded as the visible surfaces of 3-dimensional bodies, but, now, the colour surface, itself, was given indepent value.

It was a Swiss who lives in France and calls himself Le Corbusier, who was to lead the way to a new architecture. Le Corbusier is also a painter and in the 'twenties he was a cubist. He is also a very talented writer and in his articles and books has successfully propagated his ideas. When, in 1925, Paris arranged an exposition of modern industrial art and interior decoration, Le Corbusier was the only one who had anything new to say. In the exposition he had erected a complete flat of the type which he believed should be found in skyscrapers. Hitherto, habitations had been designed to give the impression of safe refuge from the world outside, of cosy comfort. Le Corbusier's abode was meant to give a feeling of contact with the outer world, the blue sky and green trees. All smaller rooms were grouped round one large room that was two storeys high and entirely open on one side. This loggia was the garden where the inhabitants could sit outdoors and still preserve privacy; a garden high up in the air. Every room had a long row of windows stretching across the entire width of the outer wall so that there were no dark corners indoors. The entire flat was as light and clean as a hospital. The home was no longer to be a museum or a burdensome testimonial of the financial standing of the occupant, but a rationally organized dwelling which would fulfil the demands of modern man.

Le Corbusier: Sketch. An architectural Fantasy with outdoor room with view over green fields.

According to Le Corbusier these demands are, first and foremost, light and air, freedom of motion, and a lovely view. It is an abode for a generation that loves sport — and particularly relaxation after sport; a generation exempt from the heroic posturing of the people in Raphael's paintings. Here, there are no classical columns to wander among; instead, there are low chairs in which to stretch out comfortably and enjoy the sight of floating clouds and leafy trees. Le Corbusier is not inspired by any period architecture but by the deck of the great ocean liner with its long row of windows, low deck-chairs and open view. Nothing is allowed to obstruct the view.

Reinforced concrete helps him to carry out his ideals. The old idea of houses in which the supporting element is illustrated by columns and the supported by architraves and beams, he dispenses with, entirely. Now, houses can be built with an inner system of pillars which support horizontal slabs of reinforced concrete. The floors of the house are the "architraves", jutting out beyond the pillars. They are like balconies that have been enclosed in glass and light outer walls which are merely to give protection against the elements and not to support any structure.

Prior to Le Corbusier, many buildings had been constructed with an interior supporting skeleton, either of steel or reinforced concrete. But this framework had been carefully hidden and the building given the appearance of a massive stone structure.

Sketch by Le Corbusier.

There are many ways of making a building appear more solid than it actually is. One method is to provide the outer walls with heavy stone quoins which form the angles of the building. These rugged, interlocking stones give the impression of great wall thickness — which does not exist. Wall-openings can be treated with equally heavy rusticated blocks which seem to say: "The wall is so heavy that this opening can be closed only by a very great effort." Huge blocks of rusticated masonry in the lower part of walls and boldly projecting cornices also give an unusually massive and rugged appearance to buildings. But just as it is possible to make a house appear much more solid than it actually is, it can also be made to appear lighter than it is.

This is what Le Corbusier does. The upper edge of a glass window in one wall corresponds with the lower edge of a balcony on another wall. The planes glide into each other as if the whole building were a house of cards. But, naturally, even the thinnest reinforced concrete construction must have *some* thickness. However, it is possible to give an illusion of planes without thickness by painting each one a different colour and letting them all meet at a corner. Both in Paris and in Copenhagen houses can be found with gables which, though they rise above the neighbouring buildings, do not give the impression of being heavy structures when they are painted with large advertisements of a different colour from the

Sketch by Le Corbusier.

façades. It is almost impossible for the observer to see these many different colour-planes as a single body. Le Corbusier, who has utilized the lessons taught by wall advertisements, camouflage painting and cubism, in his architecture, has made some of his buildings marvels of colour-combinations, with the result that they seem absolutely weightless. They are even lighter than aeroplanes and bicycles. All magnificence, all impressiveness, all redundancy has been done away with.

Le Corbusier is a great admirer of machinery. He has said that 'the house is a machine to live in' and this has been interpreted as a tendency toward a purely functional art, a completely prosaic, mechanical construction. But, according to Le Corbusier, the machine expresses the rhythm and poetry of our time, and his desire is to create something poetic, something beautiful. This is evidenced by his lovely drawings. He reveals the ecstasy of a Jules Verne over the wonders of technology but it is, above all, from the art of painting that he draws his inspiration.

He wants dwelling houses located so that there will be a fine view from every window. In 1942, when working on his stimulating book "La Maison des Hommes", he casually glanced at the wall paper in his hotel room and discovered that it was, as he tells us, "entirely delightful, the embodiment of a world from which chaos had been banned and where desire had not yet been born". And suddenly he sees in Absolut-

193

Detail from an old French wall-paper reproduced in Le Corbusier's book "La Maison des Hommes."

ism's romantic flight from reality, in the heroic landscape, his own ideals. This enjoyment of the purely visual, the pleasures of passive observation, is very different from the English ideal — to give everyone the opportunity to lead an active life.

This passive pleasure of enjoying a fine view from every window would never satisfy the more active Englishman. His ideal is a house with a garden, in which he can plant and prune and, indeed, himself make the view to be had from his window. In 1898, Ebenezer Howard proposed plans for a garden city which would unite the advantages of city life with the pleasures of the country. Le Corbusier, despite all his modernism, carries on the ideals of both the Paris of the monarchy and of Napoleon III. He plans to make it a still more wonderful, still more modern city, with high houses very much better than Hausmann's and surrounded by parks that are just as capricious and romantic as Alphand's. Howard, who was something of an inventor, wanted to experiment with the ideals *his* countrymen had always had — the one-family house, near a village green and with easy access to open country. He did not believe in big cities but thought they should be separated into small, easily manageable communities, a cluster of small towns, each with its full measure of social life and institutions; in other words, that which London, really, always had been. Both Le Corbusier and Howard avoid the dreary grey tenement houses of the 19th century. They are both reformers but each one reforms from his own point of view, — one French, the other English.

Plans for ideal cities were published in England throughout the entire 19th century. The best known is the town of Bournville, which the chocolate manufacturer, Cadbury, founded in 1879 near his Birmingham factories.

Ebenezer Howard's plan of 1898 was for the establishment of new, independent towns, not connected with any one man or industry. All land was to be owned by the community and the inhabitants were to be self-governing. Here, too, the size of the town was to be limited — Howard suggests 30,000 inhabitants — and, like medieval towns, it was to be surrounded by an agricultural belt covering an area five times as large as the urban district. There was to be no discord between town and country; the two should be closely allied. The agricultural belt was to be large enough to provide the town with fresh foods and dairy products. Howard was eager to have everything carried out with as little transportation as possible. This does not mean that he was opposed to modern technique; on the contrary, he was eager to employ it, and had visualized (in the 1890s!) factories driven by electricity to avoid the smoke plague! But he conceived the entire town as one great enterprise, functioning with the least possible loss of time and energy, and saw no reason for using intricate machinery to do things that could be done easily and simply by preliminary planning, alone. Just as the town was to have its own agricultural belt, it was also to have its own, properly located, industries, so that the inhabitants would have the shortest possible distance between home and place of work. The town was to have its cultural institutions and everything else necessary to give the inhabitants all the advantages of city life although they lived in rural surroundings. Howard believed that, to be able to carry out his plans, it was absolutely necessary to prevent any possibility of land speculation. The inhabitants were to pay a yearly rate for the use of the land and the money was to go to the community as a whole.

We get some idea of Ebenezer Howard's entire mental make-up when we hear that he did not employ his time spreading the gospel of garden cities in the abstract. But he did work energetically to get just one garden city started. The most important thing for him was to have his ideas realized in one place so that a study could be made of the way people developed when they were given other opportunities than those offered by existing cities. In his little book on garden cities there were no enticing illustrations showing how wonderful it would be, no description of how much healthier to live in a garden city than in a huge, modern town. But there were a number of statements showing how the financing would be carried out and how the town was to pay for itself. His only illustrations were several schematic diagrams. One of them was set up as three magnets, one listing the attractions of town life, another of country life, and the third showing how the garden city combines the advantages of both. Another diagram showed city types of the future, as Howard saw them. Instead of great cities, spreading out more and more, with occasional green

This rock near Rio de Janeiro is famous.

Wild mountains rise up around it, the sea foams over it.

Palms and banana trees, the glamour of the tropics brightens the landscape, you place your armchair in position.

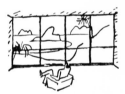

Bang! A frame appears. Bang! The four slanting lines of the perspective. Here you have an unimpeded view from your window. The landscape comes right into your room.

Typical drawings and texts by Le Corbusier from his book "La Maison des Hommes". They reveal in a striking manner his interest for the passive enjoyment of the beautiful picture in contrast to the active pleasure the Anglo-Saxon seeks in his leisure hours through sports and other activities.

195

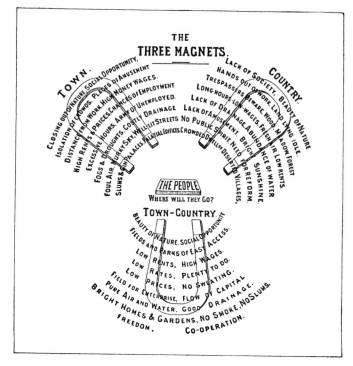

Diagram from Ebenezer Howard's book: "To-morrow", from 1898. It illustrates the advantages and disadvantages of country life and town life and offers as the third possibility the garden city which combines the advantages of the first two.

oases in the midst of the urban development, he conjures up a vision of a planetary system of small towns around the original town, separated from each other and the older city by green belts and connected by easy transport routes. The one-family house is by no means a *sine qua non* of garden cities. The inhabitants can decide for themselves how they wish to live. Indeed, it was Howard's express desire to create a city in which everyone would have a chance to arrange his life according to his heart's desire. In any case, types of dwellings were not to be determined by what would be of greatest profit to speculators. Nobody who wished to live close to the earth, with a garden of his own, was to be forced to live in a tenement house.

Howard actually succeeded in getting the necessary number of influential people interested in his idea and in 1902 the "Garden City Co. Ltd." was formed to carry out his plans. In 1903, the first garden city, Letchworth, was started. It was located near a railway, about 40 miles from London. By 1917 it had grown large enough to be incorporated and have its own municipal council. In 1920, the second garden city, Welwyn, was established somewhat nearer London. Shortly

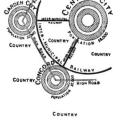

Planetary town system suggested by Ebenezer Howard in 1898.

before the outbreak of World War II these two garden cities had 18,000 and 15,000 inhabitants, respectively. Here, for the first time under modern conditions two new, independent towns have been built up on new sites, just as in the Middle Ages. These two garden cities are by no means a sort of permanent outdoor exhibition of model towns but real urban communities, with large and small industries and a full measure of social life for their inhabitants.

While it had been Howard's aim to start just one garden city as an experiment and then study the results and profit by them, others took up the idea of breaking up large cities into planetary systems and immediately saw in it a cure-all for the ills of society. While Howard soberly described the advantages of arranging the practical functions of a town so that unnecessary transport could be avoided, others have built up an entire philosophy purporting to prove how much happier and more virtuous people would become by living in small, well-balanced communities, where they could take an interest in each other, instead of in great cities where they were only cogs in the wheels of the gigantic machinery, lonely and egoistic. The fact that a steady stream of people poured into the large cities, apparently preferring them to small communities, made no impression on these garden city prophets.

There is something in the whole idea of the garden city that is deeply rooted in English mentality, in the English way of life, and in English political life. British members of Parliament, for example, are in much more intimate contact with their constituents than is usual in most other countries. Local government, which has played so important a rôle throughout English history, easily becomes a caricature of itself in mass communities. During the ascendancy of the dictators in the 'thirties, there were people both in America and in England who were convinced that the best safeguard against the mass suggestion then witnessed in Germany would be the subdivision of society into small communities where everyone knew everyone else.

The Second World War was to give further impulse to the garden city idea in anglo-saxon countries, where it became almost a gospel. The appalling destruction of English cities confronted English town-planners with inordinate problems.

They were well aware that a long time must elapse before reconstruction could begin and they could create the cities of the future. But it was of vital importance to give the people something pleasant and encouraging to look forward to when the horrors and hardships of war had finally ceased. What could be a better prospect than an idyllic cottage in a lovely garden city where all classes lived together in peace and harmony? This was in keeping with the general tenor of the day. The war was teaching people two things: first, the value of a solidarity which recognized no social barriers; and, secondly, liberation from the bonds of tradition. Under the great pressure from the outer world arose the same sort of co-operating groups and good neighbourliness that had existed in the cramped, walled cities of the Middle Ages, the sort of life which garden city prophets claimed to be the ideal. All classes mingled in war work, and people who, under normal conditions, never would have met, were being thrust together in air raid shelters where they learned to respect each other. Whole districts were suddenly changed to a mass of ruins, and this helped to rid people of old notions of the inevitability of the traditional type of city. The human estate became more important than real estate.

While bombs did their destructive work by night, town-planners worked during the day to create ideal prospects for the morrow. In the course of but two years, a gigantic plan for the London of the future was worked out. The great, scattered city was to be divided up into small units separated by green belts while outside the city, at suitable distances, new "satel-lite" towns were to be created according to the very newest ideas. The plans were published in a handy volume with a well-written text setting forth all the problems involved and with many excellent illustrations — photographs of the best from the past and alluring prospects of what was to come.

It is, indeed, the irony of fate that ideas proposed by Ebenezer Howard, a man who believed in freedom and individuality, have been standardized into a system used by English town-planners, in season and out. Post-war conditions have made it difficult for England to fulfil the promises for the future made during the war. As soon as the pressure of war was over, the old class barriers were raised again and the desire to live in small, class-less communities diminished alarmingly. Thus, while English town-planners consider it their goal to create small communities where people can live in close contact with the soil and where children can profit by the amenities of the garden, the small school and the playing field, Le Corbusier, is building *his* ideal community in Marseille — a whole town of 2,000 inhabitants housed in a single building erected on piers. It is to be a skyscraper with an unrestricted view from every window, in which the residents can dine at a co-operative restaurant and make their purchases in the shops lining the "shopping street" high up in the building, midway between heaven and earth. All two thousand inhabitants will live along corridors that lead to the lifts which swiftly can bring them up to the roof gardens or down to their cars in the parking space under the building. Everything has been worked out for them, artistically as well as technically — except how children are to develop in such surroundings.

In the English garden city and Le Corbusier's skyscraper we have a new version of "A Tale of Two Cities".

During the war the scarcity of all kinds of material forced many countries, including Denmark, into more conservative building methods, employing brick and timber where, before the war, concrete and steel had been used. In many places, too, architects have lacked the imagination to take advantage of the freedom Functionalism provided and, fearing simplicity, have returned to a more traditional building method and all the expedients of the past. But in the long run modern civilization will create so many building problems which cannot be solved by the heavy, representative architecture of the past, that architects will be forced to learn to use the freedom Functionalism has proclaimed.

INDEX